Megan McKenna

THE HOUR OF
THE TIGER

Facing our Fears

An Corp. parish

be filled with Courage
+ fear of the Lord.

Peace,
Megan

VERITAS

First published 2008 by
Veritas Publications
7/8 Lower Abbey Street
Dublin 1
Ireland
Email publications@veritas.ie
Website www.veritas.ie

ISBN 978 184730 079 9

10 9 8 7 6 5 4 3 2

Lines from T.S. Eliot, Four Quartets, 'East Coker' courtesy of Harvest Books, 1968 (p. 29); lines from 'The Great Hunger' by Patrick Kavanagh are reproduced from Collected Poems, edited by Antoinette Quinn (Allen Lane, 2007), by kind permission the Estate of the late Katherine B. Kavanagh, through the Jonathan Williams Literary Agency (p. 61).

Scripture quotations are from *New American Bible*, copyright 2002 © by United States Conference of Catholic Bishops

Designed by Paula Ryan
Cover image courtesy of Getty Images
Printed in the Republic of Ireland by Betaprint, Dublin

Veritas books are printed on paper made from the wood pulp of managed forests.
For every tree felled, at least one tree is planted, thereby renewing natural resources.

CONTENTS

for Margaret with deep gratitude and love
and for all those who have the hidden heart of a tiger within

INTRODUCTION

No heaven, no earth, just this mysterious place we walk in dazedly …[1]

This book might appear to be about fear, since that word appears in the title. Or it might be about tigers, since that word also is there, and there are many tiger stories in the book. In fact, this book is about the present moment – every moment – and about the word 'facing'. It is about facing life and death; about facing fear and love, about facing all the hard issues of life and all the mysterious deep places of living too. There is a short poem by a Chinese Zen monk, Qing Tian, that can serve as an introduction to this book and its reflections:

> Late autumn rain is a rain of mist
> tiger tracks appear in the moss
> the west wind doesn't stop all night
> by dawn yellow leaves are up to the steps.[2]

In Asia and in Zen poetry the season of autumn is the time of fullness, maturity and old age. It is also the time for letting go, for reflecting upon life and the passage of time and turning to face death – one's own eventually and the dying of all things. The rain in many cultures is a symbol of blessing, rich and soaking, like the 'soft' rain of Ireland or the fierce rains that

---

1. Megan McKenna.
2. From *The Zen Words of Stonehouse*, trans., Bill Porter (pen name of Red Pine), Mercury House, 1999.

1

come upon the desert in spring. It is considered the grace and presence of the Holy when it rains on your birthday, wedding, anniversaries and the day of your funeral. It is a rain of mist – that weather phenomenon that shrouds all in haze, imparting a sense of mystery and the unknown to all the world. Into this natural setting comes the sight of tiger tracks left on the moss, imprinted in the still moist ground. It seems the tigers of China were small but, like all tigers, could roar, and so they were used as a synonym for the wind's roaring in the trees. It is the wind that shakes the leaves free of their tight hold on the limbs of the trees; and the presence, maybe even just the thought, of a tiger in our midst would be enough to shake us loose of whatever we were involved with at any moment. The whole feel of the poem is mysterious, as if one has stepped into a place of unknowing where things are in flux and disarray. There is the sense that there is a great deal of movement in all aspects of nature and that that energy and shifting slips into the person who has stepped into the scene. And yet the last line is serene, another note on what is and has happened – the leaves have piled up on the steps. In some ways this moment describes what is intended with this book's content and topic.

The tiger is often referred to as the lion of Asia, the king and queen of the beasts. When I have seen tigers in Southeast Asia I am fascinated by how they are strong and enormous, yet lithe and sensuous. They can move incredibly fast and yet they usually move almost languidly, silently through the jungle growth. I have watched them rip meat from bones and tear other animals into pieces with ferocity, unaware they are being observed. I was brutally and suddenly reminded of being on the bottom of the food chain in the wild. Poet William Blake describes a tiger as possessing 'fearful symmetry'. This is how they are described in Elizabeth Caspari's *Animal Life in Nature, Myth and Dreams:*

> ... the tiger is so perfectly camouflaged in the dark and
> dappled jungle light that it can evoke apprehensive
> trembling over lurking, shadowed, sudden death ... At
> home in the jungles of India, the mountains of Tibet, or
> the taiga of Siberia, tigers require only water, shelter
> and an adequate supply of large prey .... Males do not
> involve themselves with raising cubs; the female, which
> is considered one of the most dangerous animals in the
> world when protecting her young, does that. Despite
> her zealous guardianship, however, only one out of three
> cubs will survive to maturity ...[3]

In legend and folk tale, as well as in teaching stories, the tiger
is the master, the teacher usually, and though it is strong and
can be vicious, it is most often met with a child or someone
who acts unexpectedly. Just as the lion lies down with the
lamb and the child sits at the entrance to the snake's den, so a
child and a tiger can be companions. This is in contrast to the
fact that tigers generally evoke in human beings emotions of
fear, terror, violence and the threat of being attacked, maimed,
killed and eaten. In the East the tiger is a symbol of power and
one of the four great creatures: the other three being the
dragon, the phoenix and the tortoise. The white tiger, the
symbol of autumn, rules the cardinal direction of the West. It
personifies the constellation of Orion, which is most clearly
seen in autumn night skies. Tigers are painted on the walls of
cities and of houses and temples to keep danger away, and
people wear tiger charms to keep disease and harm away. I
was shown a tiny pair of children's shoes elaborately
embroidered with tigers for protection, and I have seen toys
and pillows, clothing and pictures of tigers everywhere. The
tiger not only protects the poor and the weak from harm and
evil, but does battle in their name and is also considered a
defender. It is a high honour in China to call a general a tiger
and his followers tiger soldiers. The Chinese god of wealth,

3. From a study guide on the film *Two Brothers* (the story of two tiger cubs separated after hunters
    intrude upon their world, written and directed by Jean-Jacques Annaud, 1989), by Frederic and
    Mary Ann Brussat, 2004, found on www.spiritualityandpractice.com.

Chao Gongming, is often riding a black tiger. In Daoism, the First Master of Heaven, Zhang Daoling, rides a tiger as he escorts the dead to their final destination. There is a famous place called Dragon-Tiger Mountain in Nanchang (Jiangxi Province), which is the legendary palace of the head of the Daoist religion. Along with the dragon, the tiger is one of the rulers of sky and earth. The tiger is considered proud and honoured for its power, strength and royalty.

Religiously one rides a tiger to show the ability to overcome evil in Hinduism and Buddhism. In rural areas, the tiger was considered to be God, especially in heavily forested areas of India. In many religions, including Islam, tigers were considered messengers sent by God to punish evil-doers. The God Shiva rides a tiger and wears a tiger-skin robe in his role as destroyer. In ancient history only nobles were allowed to hunt the tiger, and kings set aside huge reserves so that the tiger could have enough space to live and raise their young. There are paintings and drawings of Buddhist monks sleeping with tigers on the inside walls of temples to teach that those who faced their fears could overcome and even tame the mystical forces of nature.

Today tigers are an endangered species and have disappeared from many of their native habitats. Tigers have been maligned as man-eating but in reality they instinctively avoid human beings. It is only when their habitat is infringed upon and the game they need to hunt for their survival is curtailed that the balance between what is predator and what is prey becomes upset and tigers turn and attack humans.

When more and more domesticated animals are available and there is less and less wild prey, tigers attack and become used to eating humans. Since they already have the characteristic of seeking out the most defenceless target in herds – the elderly, the sick and the young – they do the same with humans. It is said that in recent decades tigers have killed more humans than any other cat.

Introduction

Of all the cats – African, Asian, Siberian, South China, Sumatran and Indo-Chinese tigers – there are only about 5,500 left in the wild. In this century their numbers have been reduced by 95 per cent. They suffer from loss of habitat and large prey to hunt, poaching and selling of their body parts on the black market, mostly for use in traditional medicine. Tigers only live less than fifteen years in the wild if they have space and are not hunted. They survive solely on meat, usually deer, boar, wild pigs, water buffalo and small mammals. They ambush their prey, but even though they are good hunters – they have to be in order to survive – they are only successful at taking down their prey about 10 per cent of the time! Thus they need sufficient prey and territory. They travel between six and twelve miles a night – they are nocturnal creatures, usually solitary, only rarely hunting in packs. They can leap more than thirty feet in a single jump, they can climb trees and swim for miles. And they can disappear in an instant in the jungle, high grasses and brush. This is why they are considered both so dangerous and so mysterious.

This magnificent creature, at the top of the animal kingdom, could be extinct in the wild in the next fifty years. To paraphrase William Blake's haunting image: tigers are not 'burning bright in the forests of the night'.

Tigers are an apt image for human beings who face their fears instead of becoming part of a herd that panics and runs, easily frightened by others who seek to manipulate fear for their own ends. But I picked the tiger because of its mysteriousness and its illusiveness and its being so unknown. It is a mystery in itself and its presence pushes us to the edge of mystery, forcing us to delve into other layers of life and death. The tiger, on the edge of extinction, tells us that we must move to the margins and approach the gates of mystery so that we can live fully human lives. But there are so many places in the world where there are no tigers! Ireland, Europe and North America have no wild tigers, though there are cats like the puma, the panther, the bobcat, and the lynx, among others, in the United Sates and Canada, and small cats in most countries. But every culture and nation has an animal that conveys the sense of the tiger – its wild beauty, otherness, power, strength and interplay with humans.

Somehow catching a glimpse of this animal pulls one towards awareness, to the edge of mystery. It is often accompanied by a strange admixture of heart-racing fear and clear attraction.

For some people in the United States and Canada, the sight of a deer, an elk or a moose standing still and looking at you can elicit such awe. I remember one early morning – around 4 a.m. – I was looking out a window on the third floor of a school I was staying at. I was startled and shocked to see a large urban fox darting across the lawn. At breakfast I had to check out what I had seen and confirm that such a creature still found places to live in the heart of the city.

The horse, especially in Ireland and some other countries, is that symbol that evokes many of the characteristics of the tiger – its solitariness that attracts; its strength and power; its ability to run and leap; its being ridden; the lure to stand face to face with it, in spite of its size. I was recently introduced to the story of Columba and the white horse who came to him before his death, found in *The Life of Columba* by Adamnan in the section called 'The Visions: Of the passing to the Lord of Our Holy Patron Columba'.[4]

When the time of Columba's dying draws near he is an old man and yet his community is reluctant to let him go and his attendant, Diormit, mourns his coming death and is inconsolable. So Columba tells him that he will give him details of his dying that no one else will know. He tells him that he will die on the Sabbath and go to his rest, and it will be at midnight that he will answer the Lord's invitation. Then, after talking with Diormit in the barn, he goes off by himself and sits down halfway between the barn and the monastery. And here the white horse comes to him.

4. Also known as Columcille, born 7 December 521, probably in County Donegal, and died in the early hours of 9 June 597 AD on the Isle of Iona, where he set up his monastery and was the first abbot.

And while the saint sat and rested there a little while, being weary with years, as I said above, behold, there came to meet him a white horse, that obedient servant which used to carry the milk-vessels between the cow pasture and the monastery. It went up to the saint and, strange to tell, put its head in his lap, inspired, I believe, by God, from whom every animal has understanding and such perception of things as the Creator Himself has bidden; and knowing that its master would soon depart from it, and that it would see him no more, it began to lament and like a human being, to shed streams of tears over the saint's bosom, weeping and foaming profusely. When he saw this, the attendant began to drive the tearful mourner away, but the saint forbade him, saying, 'Let it be, as it loves us, let it be, that it may pour out into my lap here the tears of its most bitter lamentation. See, though you are a man and have a rational soul, you could have known nothing of my departure except what I lately disclosed to you myself: yet to this brute and unreasoning beast the Creator Himself has clearly revealed, in His own chosen way, that its master is about to depart from it. And saying this, he blessed the horse that served him, as it turned away from him in sorrow.[5]

The story is touching, a marvel, and whimsical in its description. But it highlights the connection between someone who has lived truthfully, courageously and faithfully, and all creation, even the animals that share earth and sky, and life with us. There are certain things one only learns with life, with facing all the fear and goodness that there is in living and in facing it all with courage and grace. Columba's wisdom extends to all creation. He then stands up, when the horse leaves him, and looks over the monastery and the island and blesses it in that moment and for the future. Then he goes to

5. *The Life of Columba* by Adamnan, abridged and translated by John Gregory, Floris Books, 1999, pp. 54–5.

7

his hut in the monastery grounds and spends his last hours copying a psalter. He stops at the thirty-third psalm where he wrote: 'They that see the Lord shall want no manner of thing that is good.' He said, 'Here, at the end of the page, I must stop'.

The next line, to be taken up by the one who succeeds him and to be penned and read by all who read his last words is this: 'Come, ye children and hearken unto me; I will teach you the fear of the Lord.' This prayer and blessing on fear – the fear of the Lord as opposed to all servile and demeaning fear – is the beginning of wisdom in every age. Fear diminishes us, paralyses our physical bodies and drains our psyches and souls. It turns us to stone, cramping and tightening our hearts, reducing us to despair, rage and violence in retaliation and frustration. We begin to fear others, to fear change, to fear life itself and we think only of killing the tiger and so killing imagination, the power of goodness and strength, wildness, freedom, hope and balance in our life and world. Fear of the Lord allows us and teaches us to face the tiger, make friends with the tiger, enter the tiger's gate, learn to see and appreciate with awe the tiger and practise some of the tiger's behaviour. We can learn to purr like the tiger, lie in the sun like the tiger, hide when necessary and live with the fierce passion of the tiger. We can enjoy the expansiveness and spaciousness of the tiger, its freedom and its gracefulness. We can learn from the tiger that the vastness of fear is nothing in relation to the universe of communion and the balance of all things. We can learn to feed the tiger its prey so that it does not turn on other prey – humans. Perhaps we can even learn to ride the tiger and sleep with the tigers curled around us, safe with the tiger cubs, and like the child of yore live the mystery of lying down with the tiger and sitting close to it – the undying image of the peace of the kingdom of God.

Jesus the child of God, the prophet, was a tiger. Jesus and Columba, the pilgrim and monk of the sixth century, were known to another monk of this century, Thomas Merton. He tells this story in his journal.

Once upon a time there was a tiger with three young cubs. They were young and playful, but the mother tiger was trapped and killed. Eventually two of the cubs died but the other one wandered, eating grass and trying to survive. It came upon a meadow filled with sheep and goats, and even though it was very hungry he ate grass with them and settled down. He would butt heads with them, roll on the grass and sleep with them. And he grew stronger and larger. He was always hungry. Sometimes he would catch a small creature and chew contentedly on it. And sometimes he would look at those around him: sheep and lambs and goats and wonder what they'd taste like – but they were already like kin to him.

Then one day a tiger appeared on the hill and the goats and sheep bleated and ran in terror, but the cub stayed. It watched as the tiger loped down the hill so graceful, so strong and free, and fast! They stood and faced each other, full grown tiger and small cub. Then the cub thought to play and put down its head and butted the tiger! The tiger looked at it and took its great paw, pulled in its claws and batted the cub, sending it rolling over the grass. The cub was stunned, but did it again. This time the tiger batted him harder and he rolled farther. A third time he put his head down and ran for the tiger. This time the tiger pulled out his claws and gently but firmly hit the cub. The cub crouched and whimpered. The tiger went and picked it up in her mouth, as tigers carry their young, and walked off with the cub in her mouth – down to the river. At the river's edge, she dropped the cub. The cub looked at itself in the water, its eyes wide. Then it looked at the tiger beside it and its eyes grew huge. It looked back and forth from the water to the tiger. Then the tiger roared, shaking the valley and filling the air, and then the cub tried it – letting out a weak growl. The tiger roared again and again, followed by the cub until they were both roaring together. Then Merton says … 'I never knew I was that tiger cub until God came mysteriously into my life and batted me once, then again and again, then picked me up in his mouth and carried me to the river that revealed to me my real nature and then I learned to roar. I think the first time I was batted by that great paw I woke up and looked at myself truthfully. The second time I got hit with that paw, claws still held in, I became a Catholic. The third time I became a trappist monk, and now every Advent and Lent I know that paw is coming and I'm to be swatted again, taken up into the mouth of God and dropped by the river's edge to once again learn to roar and to become more of what I was born to be.'

The tiger approaches us and it is up to us to face it in all its forms. Or we come upon a solitary horse in a field backlit by mist and evening shadows and we are drawn into reflection, into the eye of the tiger. All of life is a mystery and there are lots of edges and margins – tigers and horses, light, cloud, rain, mist, death, violence, war, suffering, pain, loneliness, sorrow, isolation, strangers, insecurity, others – all reeking of the mystery of the unknown and the fullness of life yet to be known, experienced, embraced and lived. It is the hour of the horse, the hour of the tiger now – it is always the hour that we are summoned with the words: Do Not Be Afraid! Come, children and hearken unto me, and I will teach you the fear of the Lord!

> We are summoned to a way of life, the way of the tiger, the way of the courageous children of God. We are invited to live with and in imitation of the Tiger of Truth, Jesus.

1 THE HOUR OF THE TIGER

FACING OUR FEARS

Everything will be OK in the end.
If it's not all OK
it's not the end.[1]

This is written on one of my refrigerator magnets. When I mention it to people, they all want to know where they can find one for themselves. Somehow it seems to give comfort, to make people ease up and even to laugh, a bit ruefully. I have thought about people's reaction to the magnet and realise that the quote and its sentiment touch a nerve in many people. It rubs against the underlying feeling of insecurity, a nameless fear and uncertainty that seeps through all of life: relationships, work, the political and economic situation, the climate of polarisation, the hype of terrorism and the vague sense of uneasiness in most human beings. Perhaps those feelings are just part of being human but they have most certainly been severely aggravated since the year 2000 AD.

The tag *'Anno Domini'* is important in describing years and the passage of time. In Western culture it implies that each year is 'the year of the Lord, *annum domino'* and that all time and all places, all things belong first and in the end to God – as do all of us who are believers. We don't usually remember that reality except towards the end of one year, the coming of the season of Advent when the Christian calendar begins another

1. Anonymous.

11

year a month in advance of the secular calendar; or at the death of loved ones and other catastrophic events. In many ways fear and time are intimately linked, for both are subtle, subterranean and shadowy.

The hour of the tiger has its roots in Asia, in the zodiac that is based on animals – the year of the tiger, the rat, the monkey, etc. – and when one is born on the earth. But it has even stronger roots in Asian meditation practices and wisdom stories of China and Japan, in the Buddhist tradition of Zen. One of the ancients is believed to have lived through the hour of the tiger regularly and it became immortalised in a teaching koan (a Japanese story, like a very short parable, that teaches wisdom).

The monk was young, inexperienced and fearful. He lived in fear of failure, of disappointing his master, of not becoming enlightened, of death and suffering, of all the illusions of his mind and the fleetingness of life. Sometimes he would sit to meditate and he would shake. Others would tease him and say he was afraid of everything, even his own shadow. But his master was wise and he suggested a remedy. First he had to face his fears. But how?

The master suggested that he move outside into the world of earth, sky and animals so that both his mind and his body would be a part of what happened. He told him of a cave high in the mountains that was good for meditating in, very isolated and private. He told him to bring water and some oat cakes and go sit, his back up against the cave wall, facing the opening, and try meditating through the night. So the fearful student diligently went to obey his master's suggestion. What the master hadn't told him was that the cave was frequented by tigers. They slept there during the day and would go out hunting at night, returning at the hour of the tiger, around 4 a.m. That hour was the darkest of the night and often the coldest part as well.

The disciple found the cave with his master's map and

settled in. He arrived just as evening came and the shadows were falling and he sat up against the wall facing the opening and he meditated. He dozed and woke fitfully. His fears came and went – about failure, about his own image and how many just laughed at him, about the future and death, and whether he'd ever be able to just live without fear. There were shadows and sounds he was not used to, even smells that assailed him, but he forced himself to stay seated. And then a tiger returned after hunting and feeding all night in the wild. The tiger was startled to find a human being (that he could smell long before he got to the cave, and moved stealthily, creeping up on him) and the young student was startled too – but he didn't know if it was just another of his illusory fears or whether it was real – an actual tiger! They were both stock still, eyeing each other. And then it dawned on the student – this was real! It was a stand-off. Minutes felt like years. The student sweated profusely, paralysed, terrified out of his mind, and didn't dare take his eyes off the tiger that was immobile, also deciding what to do.

The student remembered everything he could about tigers in the wild. He knew that if he moved and tried to run, or if he bolted, the tiger would see him as food. He wondered if the tiger had been successful in its hunt and looked more closely for signs of blood or anything that would indicate that he had eaten and may not be so hungry after all. And then another fear crept in – the cave! Did the tiger live here? Did the tiger live alone? He was aware that tigers protect their young fiercely from any harm. He hadn't had time to check out how far the cave went back into the mountain – were the tiger's cubs in the back? Did the tiger have a mate? If so, where was the other tiger? The time stretched out and he was aware that he'd never been more alive in his life. His mind and his body were alert and yet he grew ever more still, self-contained and resolute, though he had all sorts of fear rooting him to the ground. But these fears were connected to something real –

not just things his mind, his heart, his memory or his experience or lack of experience conjured up for his hungry soul.

Finally it was the tiger that moved ... very slowly. It walked past the student and back into the cave. He didn't know whether to sigh in relief, cry, crawl and see if his legs still moved, run or what. He just sat there trying to collect his wits. And then, another tiger appeared, dragging a carcass in its teeth. One of his worst fears surfaced again – the cave must be inhabited by tigers, a family of them, and this one was bringing home meat to feed the young ones! Again a staring match started. The second tiger smelled its mate and knew its young were in the cave. The student didn't move and had to learn how to breathe all over again, though this time it didn't take as long. Again the tiger moved first and padded past him back into the recesses of the cave. The student didn't move and before he knew it, he fell asleep from sheer exhaustion.

When he awoke it was dusk again and what awoke him was the two tigers walking past him, tight against the wall of the cave, out into the small clearing. When they had left, he moved. He went and washed the sweat off himself at a nearby stream, drank water and then sitting on a stone he realised he had to make a decision. After a moment or two, he went back to the cave, got himself settled in the same spot, sat down and began to mediate, knowing this time the tigers would return. And this became his routine. He would leave the cave when the tigers did and bathe, drink, have something to eat, and then return at around midnight. Then he would meditate and wait for the hour of the tiger – when the animals would return and they both would face off and look at each other. Always the tigers would walk past him and he would sit in his fears and trembling and yet not leave, and then he would sleep, from exhaustion, exertion and exhilaration. The days and nights passed. Nothing changed – except for one small detail. It took him many nights to realise that the tigers were inching closer and closer to him, sniffing at him and coming within a hair's breath of his face, his body. A slight movement and he could reach out and touch them if he wanted to.

On occasion a tiger would lie down next to him and go to sleep. Then another one would lie down, then another, followed by the smaller tigers, until they were all sleeping together. After months of these nights, the student knew he could go back to his own world. He could and did know how to face his fears. Surprisingly he had learned to love the tigers and he knew that he would miss their company, their presence and all that they had taught him simply by being what they were – tigers. And so one evening when the tigers went to hunt, he went back to the city, to his master and to the others. The master was waiting for him, with a knowing smile on his face.

This is a story but it is foundational and based on a reality every human being faces – that hour of the tiger, between the hours of 3 a.m. and 5 a.m., more precisely 4 in the morning. When I tell this small bit of information to people there is always a knowing look on their faces. When others mention it in their classrooms or talks everyone responds – they know the hour of the tiger, though they perhaps have never named it as such. They sometimes awake just around this time, in the darkest and coldest part of the night, alone, and they have to face themselves. They experience a sense of distress, of vague uneasiness, dis-ease or outright fear, loneliness and dread. It is the hour of the tiger – the time to face our fears. It is a common experience and necessary for every human being. Not to face those fears is to be consumed by them.

I have often wondered if Western monasticism has shared this sense of the 'hour of the tiger'. Monks rise early for vigils at three or four in the morning to pray for the world and to keep watch through the hardest part of the night, asking to be guarded through the shadows and illusions, the world's fears of what lurks 'out there', as well as witnessing to the coming of the light once again – the creator's testimony to ongoing life. It is part of the ritual of prayer, of discipline for those who are intent on living with intention, wide awake and steeped in grace's ongoing freedom.

This book would appear to be primarily about *fear*, but in reality it's about the other side of fear, which is *courage*. The dictionary definition for fear can be enlightening in itself:

> **FEAR** 1. panic or distress caused by exposure to danger, expectation of pain, etc. 2. cause of fear (all fears removed). 3. danger, 1a. feel fear about or toward (a person or thing). b. feel fear [followed by for] feel anxiety about. Fearless; adj. fearlessly; adv. fearlessness; noun.
>
> Noun:1. dread, terror, horror; fright, timidity; alarm, trepidation, apprehension. 2. horror, spector, nightmare, bogey, phobia. 3. see danger. 1a be afraid or scared or fearful or frightened, tremble, shudder. 2. see worry. **Opposite**: 1. fearless. Courageous, brave, bold, intrepid, daring, audacious.

Other expressions of fear include:

> Intimidated, jittery, nervous, edgy, cowardly, yellow, jumpy, dire, dreadful, frightful, appalling, ghastly, atrocious, terrifying, fearsome, nervous, hesitant, menacing, awesome.[2]

Our lives seem full of fear: fear of death, violence, terrorism and war, suffering and death, loss, dependence, failure, lack of control; fear of loneliness and isolation; fear of insecurity that is economic, political, religious and national; fear of the unknown, the ultimate Unknown – God; fear of the other, the stranger, the alien, the immigrant, the refugee, the sick, the

---

2. From *The Oxford American Desk Dictionary and Thesaurus*, 2nd edition, Berkeley Books, 2001.

homeless, the mentally disabled, the different whom we often label 'enemy' in an attempt to make them inhuman; fear of the weather and the universe; fear of life itself, and fear of change. I'm sure others would have more to add but this list is more than adequate when speaking of our fears. And they are 'our' fears – we share them as human beings; they are communal, plural and they are heightened and intensified when they are manipulated and used by others for control that is fabricated into hatred and expressed in action. Fear is, in a sense, natural and necessary for the human race to survive – especially when it is directed towards actual realities that are dangerous and life-threatening. However, the majority of our fears are not based in reality. They are based in our lack of faith, hope, courage and love; our ignorance and our weaknesses; our need to feel superior, to control and be independent; our need to assert ourselves, to be aggressive, to be right, to be the best (according to our very limited criteria) or to be unlike others in the human race. In the East they would say that most of our fears are illusions, fantasies or ghosts, ethereal and without substance, but they are fed regularly because we are afraid to look at the truth, afraid of ourselves or the reality around us.

Do not be afraid!
Jesus

In light of the reality and power of fear in our lives, it is interesting to note that probably the most oft-repeated line in the Scriptures of the Christian religion is the phrase *'Do not be afraid'* or a variant of those words. It is said (though I have not been able to verify it) that those words or something similar appear 366 times in the Old and New Testament – one for every day of the year and another for good measure, an extra just in case we think we need it for something altogether new and different that might crop up unexpectedly in life. We have to ask ourselves the question: are we hard-wired for fear or are we hard-wired for courage, for life? Is God the God of fear and to be feared, or is God the God of courage and life and so to be imitated with the vibrant living of life with courage and gracefulness? The word 'courage' – the antidote to fear – comes from the ancient word for heart – 'cor'. This definition opens up many possibilities for dealing with our fears.

> **COURAGE** ... an ability to disregard fear; bravery; valour, boldness, gallantry, dauntlessness, daring, fearlessness, heroism, nerve, pluck, grit, guts, audaciousness, stalwart, spunk, moxie.[3]

In a phrase, do we live with heart? This is also the core of Christian belief and the mystery of the Incarnation (God becoming flesh, blood and bone, a human being) and God in Jesus filled with the Spirit as he lived, suffered, died and was raised from the dead in the mystery of the Resurrection. Do we live and dwell in the graceful power of the Trinity, the communion and community of those who stake their life with God in flesh along with the whole human race? And do we dwell in a world that is the sacrament of the Spirit of Truth and Holiness/wholeness and Freedom as the beloved children and servants of the God of the living? Someone once told me that wherever fear dwells and rules in our lives, God does not. That staggered me and I reacted almost violently. With time's passing and experience, however, I now believe that completely. All our fears declare that God does not rule in this place, this situation, circumstance, relationship or reality – something else does. That something else reeks of death, violence and what makes us inhuman; that is bound to the worst of our choices and inclinations and shared weaknesses as human beings, lacking in faith, in grace and the Spirit of God.

In Matthew's gospel the struggling and very fearful community of disciples, both men and women, are bound and controlled by their fears. There is much to be afraid of: the

---

3. Ibid.

torture and the execution by crucifixion of their beloved master Jesus; collusion between the leaders of their religion and their occupying oppressors, the Roman empire; their own betrayals, so personal and intimate, and cowardly; their terror at what might happen to them if they are associated with Jesus and so their vehement, on occasion (see Peter), denial of even knowing him, let alone being friends with the man. They are shrouded in a climate of death, of terror at every turn, of violence and lies; and of evil – murder that is calculated, and efficiently carried out. There is the evil of a crowd whipped into a mob that is bloodthirsty and filled with anger, taking it out on a defenceless and innocent human being; a people manipulated into bringing the charge of treachery and intent to destroy a government against a single man they decree guilty of terrorism for preaching good news to the poor. And there is the evil mutilation of a man, who lives utterly without violence, in torture and death by the usual form of capital punishment, used only by the dominant forces in society on those without power.

This is the backdrop to Matthew's version of Jesus' death and resurrection. It is the story in all the gospels, but in Matthew's account, written at the time of massive persecution of the Christian community, it is told as a story of three groups of people: the Roman empire, as the occupying force in Palestine, the leaders of the Jewish priesthood and Sanhedrin, and Jesus' own timid disciples – all the men who have fled in fear and the women who watch from a safe distance. In reading the story, we must choose which group we belong to and if our actions reveal us as friends or foes or those who refuse to choose because of fear. Of its very nature, this passage reveals all of us as lacking in courage, love, freedom, friendship and faith. Jesus dies and is buried by a man who up to this point has lived in the shadows as a disciple, Joseph of Arimathea. He goes to Pilate and claims the body and buries Jesus in his own tomb. It is he who rolls the stone in front of the tomb/cave of rock while some women watch from a distance. They 'remained sitting there, facing the tomb' (Mt 27:61). This has echoes of our friend sitting at the entrance of his cave, waiting on the tiger's return.

The powers that be, both in religion and politics, are afraid too. Some of the Pharisees and the chief priests go to Pilate the next day and, through lies and false accusations against Jesus, request that Pilate do something to make sure that his disciples don't steal his body and then claim that he's alive. Pilate agrees, telling them 'the guard is yours; go secure it as best you can'. 'So they went and secured the tomb by fixing a seal to the stone and setting the guard' (Mt 27:62-66). The scene is set: fear rules in the arena of politics, in organised religion and in the land.

When morning comes, the women come to 'see' the tomb – knowing that they cannot enter because of the guard. It was the custom to come and grieve, after the Sabbath was over. The women walk in on total confusion: a violent earthquake, an angel of light and power that approaches the tomb and rolls away the stone and sits on it! 'The guards are shaken with fear of him and become like dead men' (Mt 28:4). The women are then addressed with the stirring words of hope, resurrection, unbelievable new possibilities for all life and the future, and the exhortation against fear!

> Then the angel said to the women in reply, 'Do not be afraid! I know that you are seeking Jesus the crucified. He is not here, for he has been raised just as he said. Come and see the place where he lay. Then go quickly and tell his disciples, "He has been raised from the dead, and he is going before you into Galilee; there you will see him". Behold, I have told you.' Then they went away quickly from the tomb, fearful yet overjoyed, and ran to announce this to his disciples.[4]

4. Mt 28:5-8.

Here we have the words 'Do not be afraid!' in the mouth (so to speak) of an angel. It is usually the opening line of an angel attempting to communicate and speak with human beings. I used to tell people if an angel appears and says to you, 'Do not be afraid', you probably have every reason to be scared out of your ever-loving mind! There are different kinds of fear: fear that is servile and paralysing, and fear that is close to awe and worship and that propels you into action. It is reality that must be faced.

The guards know the first kind of fear and the women know the other, which is life-giving and full of Spirit and Truth. Its effects are seeing, obeying, moving, even running, and fear that is mixed with awe and wonder – even joy! They enter the tomb and see. They listen and go forth to share what they have seen and heard with those who are not there because of their fear, their guilt and their cowardice. In their response, the women know fear that is fierce joy. In a sense this is a scriptural version of the cave, the hour of the tiger and the need to face our fears.

These words that give heart and open a door into a reality unseen and unheard of is not the end of the story. The women run in fear and expectation, overjoyed, keyed up and elated, and they run headlong into Jesus!

> And behold, Jesus met them on their way and greeted them. They approached, embraced his feet, and did him homage. Then Jesus said to them: 'Do not be afraid. Go tell my brothers to go to Galilee, and there they will see me.'[5]

It is the person of Jesus, crucified and risen from the dead, that dispels their fears. In some of the older versions of this gospel, the traditional greeting of a Jew that is also a blessing and a command is inserted into the text at this point – 'Peace be with you!' – and then the demand follows: 'Do not be

5. Mt 28:9-10.

afraid!' It is part of the proclamation of the Resurrection, the heart and soul of the gospel of God in Jesus Christ by the power of the Spirit. Jesus goes on to deepen and permeate the life and the heart of the women with what he says next: 'Go tell my brothers ...' They are his sisters in this new moment, this new day of creation, this new life that is erupting into their lives, as the earthquake shattered stone and ground, shaking angels out of heaven and opening even tombs and the earth itself to the power that is the presence of God among us. There is no need to fear, for God is so close to us as to be our Father, our Brother, our Friend and our indwelling Spirit. All is different; all is forgiven; all is injected with hope; all life now lies ahead; all living now is with courage and power.

The gospel continues with Jesus meeting with all the disciples on a mountain (and some doubt still – very close to being fearful and hesitant, unsure, insecure and slow to believe). His words are all about fear and life.

> Then Jesus approached and said to them, 'All power in heaven and on earth has been given to me. Go, therefore, and make disciples of all nations, baptizing them in the name of the Father, and of the Son, and of the Holy Spirit, teaching them to observe all that I have commanded you. And behold, I am with you always, until the end of the age.'[6]

This is the summation, the ultimate words of power that Jesus shares with all peoples on earth and especially with those who will seek to follow him in his lifestyle and obedience to the God of life that is a communion of Father, Son and Spirit and all that is created in heaven and on earth. It is about power and how to live in the world. In Matthew's gospel it hearkens back to the beginnings of Jesus' public presence in the world. He is driven into the desert by the power of the Spirit of God and is tempted, or tested, as to his intent, his identity and how he will

6. Mt 28:18-20.

use the power of God that is given to him. The last temptation regards power and what kind of power is used to bring the kingdom of God, the kingdom of justice and abiding peace for all, the kingdom of truth, of forgiveness and mercy, the kingdom of courage that is given now to the children of God in freedom and grace.

> Then the devil took him to a very high mountain, and showed him all the kingdoms of the world in their magnificence, and he said to him, 'All these I shall give to you, if you will prostrate yourself and worship me.' At this, Jesus said to him, 'Get away, Satan!' It is written: 'The Lord, your God, shall you worship and him alone shall you serve.'[7]

Now the gauntlet is thrown down. There are two ways to dwell in the world: there is the world of the devil, or Satan, whose name means 'the hinderer' and is anything or anyone that hinders us from living as human beings, fully living in the freedom of the children of God; or there is the world of what is holy, what is of God and truth, and what makes for the communion of all peoples that is based on 'no fear'! Jesus proclaims that now all power on earth and in heaven belongs to him and he gives it away freely to us to build a world made up of people from all nations that seek communion together for all. They will obey the first principle of God's domain: 'Do not be afraid!'

Sadly, most of the kingdoms of the world are based on and ruled with fear as their primary motivation. In other translations, the words of the hinderer read: 'All these kingdoms are mine and I give them to whom I wish ... only prostrate yourself before me.' The realities of the kingdoms of this world are military might, aggression and arrogance; violence, terror, torture, nationalism; threats of insecurity, lack and the fear of being dependent on others. We are told to

7.   Mt 4:8-10.

cower in fear and keep everything as it is: in our lifestyles, our relations with others and our dominance in politics, economics, religion and personal situations. This is living superficially, in fear, on the surface of reality.

We are reminded that we must only bow down in freedom and in awe, in gratitude and hope to the God of the living, the God who has been called 'I AM' for thousands of years, who is with us always, in all places and circumstances, throughout all the ages. This is a fear that is more positively known as fear of the Lord that is a gift of the Spirit; the beginning of wisdom; the ingredient necessary for wonder, discovery, adventure and risk-taking; the jumping-off place for courage and daring based on hope and ever-more abundant life and freedom for all.

Each of us, all of us, must enter caves and tombs whether they are carved out of mountains by the elements or made by humans and sit facing the openings. We must face our fears alone and with one another and then, knowing what is illusion and what is truth, we can return to our lives to actually live.

The rest of this book will look at some of our fears and sit with them in the shadow of the Scriptures until we face the tigers together so that we might go forth in obedience to the words of Jesus, 'Do not be afraid!' and perhaps bring beauty to the world that is based not in illusion or evil but in truth and goodness.

Practice
Sit alone, back up against a wall, outdoors preferably with the air close on your skin and write. Make a list of your fears on one side of a page. Write for about ten minutes. Then go back to the top of the page and change your list into a litany by reading each fear slowly, mindfully and adding next to it the words/prayer: 'O Lord, deliver me.' Then repeat it, this time praying: 'O Lord, deliver us.' End by asking that you might live out of courage and heart, grateful for the awesome reality of life.

2 FACING DEATH

Something that is yours forever is never precious.[1]

Someone once said that the beginning of facing a fear lies in naming it. This is true in regard to the fear that is perhaps the source of all the other fears: Death. Death is the obvious kind of end that each and all human beings face: the end of physical life, the end of our bodies and our presence and place in the world. But there are so many other kinds of death as well: the death of dreams, the death of a marriage, or relationship of friends; the death of others – loved ones, and even strangers who touch us unexpectedly and draw forth tears and grief that make life seem bereft and without consolation. There is death on massive scales: genocide, sectarian wars, attacks on countries that are unprovoked but deemed rational, or necessary for national security. There is death that is singular: executions, euthanasia, random drive-by shootings, accidents, drunk drivers, abortions, rapes, long-buried landmines and bombs, long vendettas over tribal, national and religious disagreements. There are deaths triggered by acts of violence and deaths that just happen to those who seem to be young and healthy. And there are deaths that seem to take forever for the old. There is the death of belief and the death of hope, called despair, depression and hatred. There are deaths that come as release after long illnesses and deaths from unknown sources,

1. From a Canadian film called *Lies My Father Told Me*, directed by Ján Kadár, written by Ted Allan, 1975.

epidemics spread by airborne bacteria, animals and birds that trigger fear and reactions that seek to stop them in their tracks before they can get to us. But no matter what kind of death, it always reeks of the end, the fear of annihilation and the futility of the desire to cling to life, whether or not life has meaning.

I often ask people what is the opposite of death and they immediately answer back: LIFE! But that is the wrong answer. The opposite of death is birth, and what happens in between those two realities or moments is what is called 'life'. In some way, death is the fullness of life, the culmination of all that has been experienced and absorbed in a period of time in our bodies, minds, hearts and spirits. For many people it is another form of birthing if one believes in a form of immortality, in something of us that is our essence and that lives on after our physical death.

Many people I work with and have the honour of being with, die lingering deaths of incurable disease that wreaks havoc and destruction on the body but leaves the mind sharp and aware. There are those who work with people whose bodies still function very well, but their minds are elsewhere and there is diminished recognition of loved ones, of self-awareness and of reality. They all call themselves midwives and their primary care is to attend to the dying and the birthing of others into the unknown, through death and in the passages of letting go of life. They consider it a responsibility, an honour and oftentimes a gift they could never have imagined before they experienced the trust and the honesty of those who let them come with them right to the threshold of what lies ahead of them.

In this chapter we will deal with physical death, of dying and the unknown that lies out there somewhere, and all the fears that mark that fact all of us will have to face. My Nana used to say to me, 'Honey, you die the way you live – so be careful that you really are living so that you can die with everything you got and go out with grace and style'. Perhaps it is harder to live without fear than it is to die without being consumed by fear.

We begin with a story from the Middle East, from the Islamic tradition, though I've heard it told by other religious groups too, attesting to its universal power. It is often called 'An Appointment with Death'.

Once upon a time the Sultan of Arabia was seated on his throne and one of his trusted advisors and close friends came in after a hard ride, obviously in terror. The Sultan stopped what he was doing to attend to his friend. The man could hardly speak he was so afraid: 'Master, I was coming across my courtyard this morning and I saw the Angel of Death walking towards me. I'm sure it was Ariel, dressed in white. He came towards me, smiling. It must mean that my end is near. What can I do?' His master surprised him and asked, 'If it was the Angel of Death and he was coming for you, you wouldn't be standing here right now, would you? You'd have gone with him.' The man stood there paralysed and couldn't speak.

So the Sultan continued, trying to ease the man's fears. 'Look, my friend, I will tell you something I don't often share with just anyone. I speak often with Ariel, the Angel of Death. He comes and we talk. In fact, I bet you met him on his way here to speak with me. He wasn't coming for you, but to see me.' But the man would not believe him. His fear pushed him and he begged the Sultan to help him. The Sultan replied that he loved him dearly and that he would do absolutely anything he could for him, anything that would ease his terror.

'I'm sure he was coming for me,' the man said. 'He looked right into my eyes that were as keen as a knife blade. I must escape and get as far away from him as I can. O woe is me, my life is over! I am doomed! I must flee, but my horse is already spent and I won't make it far. Can you give me one of your best horses, one of your Arabian steeds that will carry me fast and far from here so that the Angel of Death will not be able to find me.' The Sultan asked him where he would go. 'I have friends in Marrakech – that's where I'll go.' The Sultan embraced his friend and ordered his fastest and most beloved horse to be saddled and brought to him. He watched his friend race off, saddened and concerned for him. Later in the cool of the evening while the Sultan was resting in his garden, the Angel of Death, Ariel, approached him. The Sultan welcomed him to the garden and told him to sit awhile and rest from his labours. They sat in silence listening to the water in the fountain and the soft wind in the branches of the trees. Then the Sultan spoke: 'Ariel, you gave one of my friends a terrible scare this morning. He saw you in his courtyard and thought you were coming for him. He must have seen you when you were on your way here to meet with me. He took fright at the very shadow of your presence.' Arial answered: 'He took me totally off guard too. I never expected to see him there in his courtyard. I have an appointment to meet with him tomorrow afternoon in Marrakech.' The Sultan sat in silence thinking of his friend and looking with knowledge and sadness at Ariel, the Angel of Death.

We avoid death. We ignore death. We refuse to look at it, to remember that we will die or to even ask questions about death. There are questions that need to be asked: if we are going to die, each of us, all of us, one day, does it impact the way we choose to live? What would prepare me for death? Will I be ready? Are any of us ever really ready to die? How can people like Francis of Assisi call Death his Sister, his companion, his friend? Could I ever refer to death, angel or reality, as a friend? How do I feel about dying?

Most of us only skirt around these questions when another dies and we are faced with our own mortality or when we have skirted the edge of danger ourselves. Poets and prophets, preachers and medical personnel quote one another on death, fearing its inevitability. There is a range of descriptions on what it is, why we die and what comes afterward. Dylan

Thomas' most oft-quoted line is probably 'Do not go gentle into that Dark ...'. A number of times I have heard lines from T.S. Eliot at wakes and funerals:

> Oh dark, dark, dark
> they all go into the dark.
> The vacant interstellar spaces – the vacant into the vacant.
> The captains, merchants, bankers, eminent men of letters
> all go into the dark ... and we all go with them
> into the silent funeral.
> I said to my soul, 'Be still
> and let the dark come upon you
> which shall be the Darkness of God.'[2]

The poet and the preacher's main task is to tell the truth and make us face reality, whether the issue is life, death, birth or all human beings' varying stages of awareness and experience of these realities. Perhaps it is not chance that puts Psalm 22 and Psalm 23 next to each other. Listen to their anguished pleas, cries of pain and ultimately cries of passionate hope:

> My God, my God, why have you abandoned me?
> Why so far from my call for help, from my cries of anguish?
> My God, I call by day, but you do not answer; by night, but I have no relief.
> You are enthroned as the Holy One; you are the glory of Israel.
> In you our ancestors trusted; they trusted you and you rescued them.
> To you they cried out and they escaped; in you they trusted and were not disappointed.
> But I am a worm, hardly human, scorned by everyone, despised by the people.

2.   T.S. Eliot, *Four Quartets*, 'East Coker'.

> All who see me mock me; they curl their lips and jeer;
> they shake their heads at me.
> 'You relied on the Lord – let him deliver you; if he loves
> you, let him rescue you.'
> Yet you drew me forth from the womb, made me safe at
> my mother's breast,
> Upon you I was thrust from the womb, since birth you
> are my God.
> Do not stay far from me, for trouble is near, and there is
> no one to help.[3]

We recognise the first line of this psalm as one of the last lines spoken aloud by Jesus in the throes of his death-agony on the cross. It cries and wrenches and clings to life that is terrible, tortured and publicly humiliating – 'like a worm' twisting in pain, not even a human being. It ends, though, with such fervent hope and a public assertion of belief that others, even if they did not hear the words from Jesus' mouth, know the words in their own minds and hearts:

> All the ends of the earth will worship and turn to the
> Lord.
> All the families of nations will bow low before you.
> For kinship belongs to the Lord, the ruler over the
> nations.
> All who sleep in the earth will bow low before God;
> All who have gone down into the dust
> Will kneel in homage.
> And I will live for the Lord, my descendants will serve
> you.
> The generations to come will be told of the Lord, that
> they may proclaim to a people yet unborn the
> deliverance you have brought.[4]

3. Ps 22:1-12.
4. Ps 22: 28-32.

It is a most unlikely ending for a prayer that began in such raw pain, so near to a violent death. The words leap from Jesus' body out into all the universe, across time and space, proclaiming worship, clinging to the God of the living and casting his lot with all humankind, saying even facing death: 'I will live for the Lord.' Jesus was born and so must die, and no matter the form of his death, he dies avowing life and the God of life who holds all human beings, even in death's grip. Jesus saw himself as belonging to a people chosen and beloved of God, and in his dying he was returning to his own people who had gone before him, in death and in life, in trembling worship and in the tremors of dying, into the mystery that is God who is Alpha and Omega.

None of these words, of course, ease the wrench and the finality of death. They are for the living as much as those who speak them as they die, but they wed death to life – life that has been lived and life that is larger than any of us individually, the life of a people, the life of the earth and the universe, and the life of God. The most profound expression of these connections I read in a homily by Dom Damien Thompson of Gethsemani Abbey in Kentucky at the funeral of a dear friend, Francis Kline – a Trappist monk and an abbot in South Carolina who was a master pianist and musician, brilliant and wise, simple and true, who died of leukaemia when he was only in his fifties. He quoted from the poem by T.S. Eliot referred to earlier in this chapter, and then went on to say:

> My friends, the words are T.S. Eliot's but the experience is each our own – to come together here, you and I, around the spent and broken body of our son, brother, friend, father, Abbot Francis. It is wrenching – death – it is soul numbing – it is so deep and vast it stretches the mind out into cavernous darkness – and it breaks the human heart. And yet – this morning, among us, his family and brothers and friends – this morning – death

itself is the Word of God written in human flesh – the flesh of our beloved Francis.

It is a loving and mysterious God decisively taking the pen from Francis' hand and finishing his life story. Death is the joining – the wedding – of the Word of God with Francis' completed earthly life.

These, most surely, are the words of believers to other believers, but it is in the face of death that belief makes sense – or gives some meaning to living, to all human beings. The tiger of death is the ultimate tiger, the ultimate fear that often abides with us as the shadow over our daily lives. And death, in so many poems, prayers and psalms, is referred to as entering darkness.

But if it is entering the presence of God, isn't it as much light as shadow? Belief, wild hope, even irrational expectation, love for life is the human, perhaps only way to face death, being birthed into another form of living and being in the presence of God. As Pascal's wager goes: better to believe and so to live as though there is a God and that God waits for us in an after-life than to wager on the non-existence of God and nothing after our life and death. As St Bernard was quoted in this homily: 'The human heart is born old and meant to grow ever younger.' Being born, being birthed by another and dying, and being birthed again are the two ultimate realities we have no control over. They happen to us, but the latter we have a great deal to do with – we leave our mark on others and the world in our living and our dying is the last word, the way we pronounce who we are and will be in others' memories and what we have staked our living on. This is our meaning, our birth pangs and the song we let echo in the world long after we are gone from this place, to the unknown, the mystery that is larger than each of us.

Psalm 23 follows the psalm of lament and we call it the Good Shepherd psalm of utter comfort, trust and being held and enclosed in the protective hand of God. 'The Lord is my shepherd, there is nothing I shall want.' We sing it and pray it often through our tears and cracked voices at the funerals of all we love and lay to rest in the ground of earth, holding onto their images, their memories and all they mean to us in life, and all that we lose in their dying. The words are for the living: 'Even though I walk through the valley of death, I fear no evil, for you are at my side' (traditional rendering). It is an acknowledgement of the past, looking back, a plea for the present and a hope for the future in the face of death's opening into what is the ultimate Unknown.

We each grieve alone, yet we all grieve together in the face of death. Psalm 22 is the prayer of the dying one and Psalm 23 is the prayer of those letting go of life and those who must face the death of others, loved and lost, but who do not die yet. Every person's death is an invitation to face a streak of our own vulnerability and the tiger of death that will come, who knows when or how or where for us. But it is stopping and facing death that is so hard – long before it is close enough for us to touch it and know it is our death. Perhaps one of the secrets of death is only found in facing it, long before it's our own up close.

Janis Joplin had a saying that was plucked out of one of her songs: 'If you're not busy being born, you're busy dying.' It is hard work being born (let alone doing the birthing!). Being born is being pushed and shoved out of one universe into another, out of one way of mostly unconscious living into another form of living that is meant to be ever-more filled with being awake, aware and conscious. Dying is about as hard as being born. We are born and so we will die. Natural death is to die of old age, worn out and spent, with your friends and relatives around you, in your own bed. There are as many ways to die as there are to be born, and so to live. Death is as much a singular part of our character as anything else we do and are as individuals.

Being born and dying

Being in a womb and a tomb are the resting places we all share initially and at the end. In the Scriptures there are two accounts of the origins and birthing of Jesus: one in Matthew that is shrouded in violence and death, and one in Luke that is shrouded in rejection and danger. Both begin in fear, occur in fear, and others experience fear and deep disturbance and distress in relation to even the possibility of this birth becoming a reality. It seems everyone in the Christmas stories is overcome with fear: Mary, Joseph, Zechariah, the shepherds, Herod and the whole city of Jerusalem. The refrain of the angels to everyone is the same: 'Do not be afraid!' All this is bound up with the birth of this child that will enter the world of history, the world of long waiting for the Jewish people who have endured long in occupied territory under the heel of the Roman empire. Every child unborn, being born and newly born is an unknown reality, an unknown factor in existence, something that can shift and alter radically all of reality.

Being born is a wild card in the universe. Being born is both a threat and a promise to all that is and is intent on living. These birth stories are trying to say: don't romanticise Christmas; don't use Christmas as a nice story that is powerless and saccharine; don't make Christmas into a time to try to escape reality, suppress your fears about life and change; don't reduce Christmas to a sweet babe in a mother's arms with a doting father in attendance, devoid of history, politics, economics, nationalism and the brutality that is a part of life too. Light only makes sense in the midst of darkness: the deeper the darkness, the more sustaining and powerful the light.

Each of the persons in the stories of the birth of Jesus is initially approached by an angel with the reassuring, confident, comforting words, 'Do not be afraid'. The word 'angel' means 'messenger', in this case a message from the Holy One. In the Christmas stories, angels, stars and dreams are all trying to make the same announcement: God is interrupting history and inserting his own presence into the world – God is coming among us as flesh and blood to share our existence, our being born, our living and our dying with us. The angel (traditionally Gabriel) comes first to Joseph.

> Joseph, son of David, do not be afraid to take Mary your wife into your home. For it is through the Holy Spirit that this child has been conceived in her. She will bear a son and you are to name him Jesus, because he will save his people from their sins.[5]

It seems so cut and dry: 'This will happen and you will do this … and it's done.' But we have to remember that Joseph goes to bed deeply troubled, having decided to put Mary 'away quietly', a euphemism for divorcing her and putting her out of the community so that she will have to fend for herself in a tight-knit society that knows everything that happens in a village. He is betrothed to her and that is a very public affair, an arrangement between families, though they are still probably living with their own families. We forget more often than not when reading these passages during the Advent season of the liturgy that this is not 'the way things happened', this is what believers forty and fifty years after the death of Jesus wrote as part of their belief in the Crucified and Risen Jesus as Lord of life and truth. There are as many stories of Jesus' genesis or origins in the human race as there are allusions to his being born, as all human beings are, as a child totally dependent on others for its survival. This is found in the angel's command that Joseph name the child Jesus – Joshua – meaning saviour of his people. In the translation it is saving people from their sins, but it could just as surely be translated 'because he will save his people from their fears'. And it is breaking with all traditions for Joseph to do the naming – that was the realm of women and their prerogative.

5. Mt 1:20b-21.

The angel Gabriel quotes Scripture, the book of the prophet Isaiah, 'and this child will have many names'. One of his more ancient ones will be Emmanuel, meaning 'God with us'; the presence of the Holy One dwelling among us. Joseph responds and obeys – he has listened and heard the Word of God and the story of this human being, God-with-us, now has a beginning. Mark's account, the first gospel written, records Jesus' life as beginning at his baptism in the Jordan by John, when he rises up out of the waters named as the beloved child and servant of the Father's voice and the Spirit's power. For Mark, Jesus is born at baptism.

We are creatures that want beginnings, middles and ends to our stories and lives. Joseph will have many dreams and words from angels; he will learn to listen to strangers from afar; watch and read the stars for meaning and he will always obey. This response is crucial, because the child is born in the midst of intrigue, a Jewish political power, King Herod, who is vicious and paranoid about his throne, killing anyone thought to be even a remote threat. We know the story – the child will be saved this time and will grow up, but another king, in collusion with the empire of Rome, will murder him, seeing him as a threat to the power he has amassed and clings to by violence.

This child's survival must be seen in the shadow of the deaths of others who do not escape the sword. The words of Jeremiah the prophet are found in the mouths of mothers and fathers lamenting the butchering of their babes in arms.

> A voice was heard in Ramah, sobbing and loud lamentation;
> Rachel weeping for her children, and she would not be consoled, since they were no more.[6]

He is saved from fear, infant genocide and collusion between religious and political leaders intent on retaining their positions of power, so that this child of God will one day save us all from

6. Mt 2:17-18, quoting Jer 31:15.

fear, genocide and collusion of religion and state. This Jesus will save us by living and dying with us and revealing to us how God lives and dies in the flesh of human beings. There are intimations from the beginning in the stories written long after Jesus' death and resurrection. They are told so that we who have been born in all sorts of circumstances will know how to live, how to save one another and then how to die as human beings.

Luke's story of the child's beginnings is told from his mother's point of view for a community struggling with a church growing by leaps and bounds throughout the empire, among rich and poor people alike. Luke takes sides in his story, having the child born in poverty, occupied territory and a climate of distrust,with people being counted in a census as though they were animals belonging to another country. The child's only bed is a manger, a feeding trough for animals, since he himself grown to be an adult will become food for the whole world. He is wrapped in swaddling cloths, foreshadowing his burial cloths, sharing the end of all peoples, as he has shared in our beginnings.

There is violence. Just as Joseph took the child and his mother and ran into Egypt as illegal aliens, sojourning there for safety, now it is the mother who runs to the outskirts of Jerusalem to shelter with Elizabeth, a distant cousin, because if she is found to be pregnant she could be stoned to death before she gives birth. We have a tendency to focus intently on Mary during Advent, Christmas and the Epiphany, but the story is about who this child is for all the world, for all peoples.

Perhaps it is the story of the shepherds that tells us about being born, and living and dying – and how fear that is always present is to be controlled and transformed as power that is good and holy. This passage is the reading at midnight mass.

Now there were shepherds in that region living in the fields and keeping night watch over their flock. The angel of the Lord appeared to them and the glory of the Lord shone around them, and they were struck with great fear. The angel said to them, 'Do not be afraid, for behold, I proclaim to you good news of great joy that will be for all the people. For today in the city of David a saviour has been born for you who is Messiah and Lord. And this will be a sign for you: you will find an infant wrapped in swaddling clothes and lying in a manger.' And suddenly there was a multitude of the heavenly host with the angel, praising God and saying: 'Glory to God in the highest, and on earth peace to those on whom his favour rests.'[7]

It is to shepherds, those who spend nights in the fields watching – their flock, the stars, their environs for danger – that the angels come announcing great joy! Joy is the antidote to fear on many occasions. What is filled with light, hope and possibility often strikes us with great fear. The birth of this child, this poor infant with no home except a cave and a manger for a cradle, this child wrapped in the cords of life and death, like all of us, is the glory of God made manifest, revealing what it means to be born, to be a human being. We are born to peace because God's favour rests upon each of us. We are birthed with God's own fullness of grace and life, God's eye and God's illimitable hope and promise for each of us. In this child we are saved from all the fears of living and all our fears of dying. We are born for joy and the praise of God.

These shepherds go in haste to see and share what they have been told with Joseph and Mary, and then they leave the child. The last we hear of them, they 'returned, glorifying and praising God for all they had heard and seen, just as it had been told to them'. That is life after the birth of Jesus who saves us from being imprisoned in our fears and terrified of the fullness of a life of joy. From the beginning, Jesus is partial to shepherds keeping watch over their flock, gazing at the stars

7. Lk 2:8-14.

and seeing God's face in a poor child born in squalor. They see through the thin veils that surround reality to the underlying joy and glory of all life, though this child will die, as will every child born to be the peace of God upon the earth.

What is there after death? Our fears are a reality and we do not know what lies after death – but we don't know what lies before us in life either. The opening line of this chapter is from a Canadian film, *Lies My Father Told Me*. It is about a young boy in a poor area of Montreal in the early 1900s and everything in his life is shifting and changing. His father keeps saying that he will come and play with him, but he's always working, too busy – he lies to him. The young boy is devoted to his grandfather, who lives with them, and the grandfather's horse that is stabled in the back yard. Late one night the boy overhears his parents talking about the fact that his grandfather is very sick and is dying, and that they must get rid of the horse. The boy is devastated. The next day he goes to his grandfather to talk and finds him brushing the old horse's coat, peacefully humming to himself. When the boy approaches he smiles at him broadly.

'Grandfather, can I ask you a question?' 'Of course, he answers.' 'I don't want you to lie to me, like everyone else does. They keep saying everything is fine, don't worry, but I want to know the truth.' The grandfather stops currying the horse and sits down next to his grandson. 'Ask me, I will tell you the truth.' 'Is the horse going to die?' He looks at his young grandson and says, 'Yes, the horse is going to die.' The next question is: 'Grandfather, are you going to die?' He looks at the boy again and says, 'I won't lie to you. Yes, I'm going to die.' The little boy begins to cry softly. 'Grandfather, we're Jews aren't we?' 'Yes, we are. Why do you ask that question?' 'Well, in all the stories we hear in synagogue there are these miracles that keep happening all the time. Grandfather, do you believe in miracles?' This time, he is slow to answer but says, 'I will not lie to you. No, I don't believe in miracles … but I have come to rely on them.' And finally, there is the last question: 'Grandfather, why does everything die?' They sit there awhile and then the grandfather says, 'I don't know. All I've learned is that something that is yours forever is never precious.' And the two of them sit together, quietly.

There must be joy, such joy, such indescribable but shared joy in our being born, our living, our dying and our being birthed into mystery, the unknown and into forever. This is the fullness of life, the reason why we are born and the way we must die.

Practice

Find a niche in which to sit and write or reflect – a place that affords you a way to look outward into the world as well as inward into your soul. Gather yourself and ask yourself these questions. How do I think I'm going to die? How would I like to die? Who do I want near me? If I have one word or phrase to say with my life – what am I saying? Once when I was teaching at a huge conference someone asked, 'How do you think you're going to die?' I was speechless and I just stood there. Then out of my mouth came words that rang true. I said, 'I think I'd like to die of gratitude.' I have remembered those words and taken them to heart every day, grateful to the person who asked me the question.

3 THE FEAR OF VIOLENCE, TERRORISM AND WAR

> At the root of all war is fear: not so much the fear men have of one another as the fear they have of everything. It is not merely that they do not trust one another; they do not even trust themselves ... They cannot trust anything because they have ceased to believe in God.[1]

Alongside our fear of death, walks the fear of violence that can attack without warning, seemingly without meaning. It can come out of nowhere in our world. And our world is rife with violence, both personal and collective, all with rational predications about its necessity and why it is being used in this situation or because of this reality. This violence is like pollution – it is in our air, our waters, the ground we walk on and our food is grown in; it is in our minds and has seeped deep into our hearts and every relationship between persons, peoples and governments. Sadly this is the backdrop and the reality of most of the world. None of our fears are groundless but we must remember that we are not constituted by our fears and that we cannot accept fear as the foundation of our decision-making. Equally we cannot listen to those who counsel violence as the primary and first response to whatever happens in our world. Fear is expressed in a long litany of how to be violent: in war, in torture, in terrorist attacks, in pre-emptive strikes, in retaliatory attacks, in plans for assassinating

1. *New Seeds of Contemplation*, Thomas Merton, revised edition, New Directions Publishing Corporation, 1972.

leaders of other countries, in the kidnapping and use of children as soldiers, in the drive for ever-more efficient weapons and in cells of people intent on lawlessness and personal destruction, and in suicide bombers.

Our fears in regard to violence are legion, whether they are rooted in governments that seek to legitimise their actions as political strategies or economic necessities (usually in regard to an unlimited flow of oil) or in the actions of small pockets of people and individuals who act out of despair, frustration or a sick mix of religious and nationalistic rationalisations. As Merton points out in the quote above, it is because people have stopped believing in God. Instead they have made idols that they worship and bow down to as the only power they will serve. For people who believe in violence and all its horrific forms, their god is destruction and death, whether or not they claim to adhere to any other religion like Christianity, Judaism, Islam etc. Their actions belie their words and reveal their worship of insatiable idols that feed on human flesh and blood sacrifice.

Since 9/11, what was already a subtle reality has become obvious: governments, countries, corporations, even religions, often use fear as their guiding principle in attempting to control their large population of members. This fear is expressed in the way laws are changed and human rights are abused, or when people are threatened with punishment. People are pushed and cowed into obeying new laws that are supposed to protect but often only make the climate of distrust stronger. There is a constant need to manufacture new enemies in order to continue plans and assert power from the least to the greatest. And *in lieu* of a specific enemy, fear uses the universal sense of insecurity to create an anonymous enemy that could be and is everyone, anywhere. Thus there must be constant vigilance and heightened levels of security alerts to keep everyone at a low-grade persistent level of fear. The enemy then deserves budgets of over 800 billion dollars a year in just one country alone to keep this terror at bay. Though there are some real dangers in the world, this fabricated 'what if' worst-case scenario can mask most of the more pressing problems and, worse, the roots of violence – those in individual lives, in nations and in the world can be glibly attributed to invisible forces intent on coming after us. The world is reduced to childish and dangerous divisions of them and us. The logic runs that we are always good, with God on our side against those who are always evil and must be destroyed.

There is a story from Africa that reveals this reality we have worked so hard to put in place and it reveals some of the motives behind our refusal to look at what is actually happening in our world – and ourselves as part and parcel of the violence. A version of the story can be found in Bennett's *Book of Virtues*[2] but this is how I tell it. I call it 'We Must Make Them Pay'.

Once upon a time there was a young leopard cub that was curious and loved to go exploring the wide world. One day on one of his trips he went far from home and the land that he knew. He wandered about and found himself right in the middle of a great herd of elephants. He was only a small leopard cub but to them he was a predator, a cat to be feared. The cub had been warned about any group of great beasts and how dangerous they could become, whether they were other cats, rhinos, hippos or, largest of all, elephants. The cub was curious, as the young are, and suddenly his presence caused great fear and the huge beasts began to run. In a moment there was a stampede and in the melee one of the elephants stepped on him, crushing him without even realising that he had killed the cub under his feet. Later that night, a hyena hunting for food came upon the dead cub and ate what was left of the small broken body.

Then the hyena went to the leopard family and began by saying: 'Don't attack me, but I bring you terrible news – I found one of your young cubs trampled to death by the

2. *The Book of Virtues: A Treasury of Great Moral Stories*, William Bennett, 1st edition, Simon & Schuster, 1993, p. 460.

elephants in the place where they gather to birth their young. There's really nothing left of him to bring back.' The parents of the cub howled, ran in circles and grieved in anger, rage and loss. They were full of questions: 'Who did it? How did it happen? Where?' They wanted not only answers to their questions but revenge. All the hyena kept saying was: 'The elephants did it. I found his crushed and helpless body in their camp.' The father kept muttering, 'The elephants, the elephants, are you sure it was the elephants?' And the hyena kept saying, 'Yes, their tracks were everywhere and it was their usual place to rest.'

The leopard knew he could not go after the elephants. He himself would be crushed. Even if he had many leopards with him, it was nearly impossible to go after one mature elephant. He turned on the hyena and screamed, 'No, you're wrong, it was not the elephants at all. It was the goats. I know it was the goats. They are always going after our young cubs, butting them with their horns and chasing them. It was the goats that murdered our young cub.' The hyena stood there speechless and the leopard ran off screaming, 'It was the goats, those dirty, stupid, aggressive goats that go after anything and everything in their greed.' He ran yelling and shouting about what the goats had done, rallying the other leopards in the area to his cause. The leopards soon found a herd of goats chewing grass in the valley not far from their hunting area and sprang on them, ripping them apart in rage. They killed as many of the goats as they could catch, leaving the field full of torn carcasses, the old and young scattered where they ran in terror, and fell under the leopard's claws and teeth.

It's an ugly story, and of course it's not about elephants, leopards, hyenas and goats, it's about human beings. It disturbs us because it tells the truth about us, to us. In so many cases, on so many occasions when we are the victims of violence, or see ourselves as the victims, we react in revenge, in frustration and rage because we want someone to pay for our grief, our loss, and we refuse to look at what has actually happened. Instead, even in the face of truth, we decide what the truth is so that we can attack something or someone that we can actually destroy. We blame and we scapegoat – figuratively, though literally in this story. And the hyena – why did he go to such lengths to inform the leopard what the elephants did, thoughtlessly, unaware of what was happening, in their own fear of a leopard cub in the midst of their young?

Often we do not deal well with truth, especially when it is intimately connected to violence. We quickly designate victim and perpetrator, rather than grieving our losses, and with others, looking at what has happened, why it has happened and where we actually fit into the larger picture. Our daily lives are saturated with constant references to acts of terrorism, people who are dubbed terrorists and whole groups of people who, in our biases, our prejudices and ignorance, are made treacherous enemies that must be immediately and completely eliminated. We make others the object of our fear and in our violent and killing reactions go after anyone, someone, to make them pay rather than grieve and suffer our loss. Worse still, we comfort ourselves with the illusion that our actions will provide us with the essential security that something like 'this' will never happen again – we've shown them what will happen to anyone who might try it. In essence what we have done is escalate the violence, extend its grasp and deepen the frustration, inequality, injustice, hatred and fear of everyone, whether they were originally involved in what happened or not – because now they are.

Fear is such a brutal force when it involves the torture, maiming, killing, execution and destruction of other human beings – for whatever reason. It matters not if it is deemed 'legal' as in matters of the death penalty – it is still unjust and evil. It matters not if it is perpetrated on one country by another country as 'necessary'. It is still, as John Paul II described it, an act of despair and disastrous for the human community. It matters not if it is explained as done in obedience to God's will, or as a religious deed, or that it is done as part of the ultimate struggle between good and evil in the world. It is always the worshipping of a false god, an idol, and each choice, each action, each blind continuance declares that the god that is worshipped is the god of death, the god that feeds on the flesh of men, women and children, the elderly and the innocent civilian or those who fight back. In the end, they are all the beloved children of the true God, the God of life, the God of the poor, the Word of God become flesh among us, and they are all equally murdered.

There is a disturbing story in Mark's gospel called 'The Healing of the Kerosene Demonic'. A man hides out in the tombs who cannot be restrained, not even with chains. He is so strong in his rage, his fear, his insanity, his grief, his self-destruction that he cuts himself with stones, night and day. Jesus crosses over the sea and comes upon the scene:

> Catching sight of Jesus from a distance, he ran up and prostrated himself before him, crying out in a loud voice, 'What have you to do with me, Jesus, Son of the Most High God? I adjure you by God, do not torment me!' He had been saying to him, 'Unclean spirit, come out of the man!' He asked him, 'What is your name?' He replied, 'Legion is my name. There are many of us.' And he pleaded earnestly with him not to drive them away from that territory.[3]

The story is laced with words and symbols that are all military in nature. The land itself was a place where many of the Roman officers retired. It was a land under occupation and the people lived with the presence of the military and all the problems that came along with economic, political and even religious collusion with the empire. Many exegetes believe that the demonic, the insane man who is harming himself and that

3. Mk 5:1-9.

cannot be contained or controlled is a symbol for war and for those who pursue military 'solutions' to all issues. The emperor of Rome considered himself a god – those very words were etched on the coins of the empire – and Rome itself was a force, politically, economically, geographically, sociologically and religiously. When the man is asked his name he replies that it is 'Legion', the largest segment of fighting forces. The man is obsessed with power, destruction, control and military might – he is, in effect, a mirror image of a people and a country that worships the false idols and gods of war and destruction.

This Legion pleads with Jesus not to drive him out of the territory, again a military maneuvering term. He suggests being sent into the swine and Jesus obliges. The Legion enters the pigs and the pigs run headlong over the hill and into the sea and they drown. Again it is the image of a stupid move that destroys an attacking force. This is a very disconcerting expulsion or setting free of someone who is imprisoned in violence, torture and strength, but the reaction of the townspeople is even more disturbing. They see the man, 'sitting clothed and in his right mind and they are seized with fear' (Mk 5:15). The very sight of Jesus who has pacified the man and brought calm and order to the whole area seizes them up and they start begging Jesus to leave their district. Why? Why does the presence of calm and peace, and the fact that someone is now in his right mind sitting with a man who questions and asks for the name of the possessed and violent and then sends them out of a region instil fear in the townspeople?

One would think that they would rejoice in the man's being released from his torture and imprisonment, and rejoice in what freedom looks like after terror and destruction. There are many kinds of fear and often those who live in collusion with destruction, with the insanity of what human beings do to others, reject what is human, what is the truth, and so reject the true nature of God that is always the presence of peace, life, those who are 'in their right mind' living without harm to others or themselves.

Jesus does leave and as he goes back to the boat, the man whom he has set free to live without violence and mutilation approaches him and pleads to be able to go with him. But Jesus is firm – no, he is to go home and tell his family and all who will listen what has been done for him, what the Lord in pity has done for him. He is to proclaim loudly and in public in all the cities of the Decapolis what Jesus has done. He is to be a preacher announcing peace and liberation from violence and fear; to be a bringer of calm and right mind by his very presence. He is to teach everyone who will listen that the work of the Lord, the work of God, the work of Jesus is peace and a life without violence, horror, torture, destruction of others, oneself and the place one dwells in. And this will cause amazement (Mk 5:11-20).

Julian of Norwich penned an almost familiar line: 'All will be well.' Thomas Merton wrote in reflection and response to this line: 'All will be well. Certainly we know that all will be well, but the ways in which God makes it well are apt to be difficult for us.' The response to violence, war and torture is a mixture of freedom that is based on justice for all, on release from what imprisons us in fear, and on hope. Hope is the virtue that is described as cardinal, meaning essential, foundational and basic to life. It is a gift and, like any gift, it can only be given to another. It isn't something we can invent, imagine or wrap up for ourselves.

There is a website called Spiritual Literacy in Wartime: Communities of Hope maintained by *Spirituality and Health* magazine. It offers practices, prayers and poetics on all the issues of the world and how to imagine and create spiritualities for all people no matter what religion they adhere to and practice. In 2004 they solicited and researched many writers', theologians' and ordinary folks' descriptions of practices of hope. Here are just two that can begin to set us on the path to living without war, violence, torture and inordinate fear of terror and mayhem.

The first is a quote from Brazilian Bishop Dom Pedro Casaldaliga: 'Prayer is hope's breathing. When we stop praying, we stop hoping.' This is so simple, so startling, and in its own way terrifying because it begins with the acknowledgement that God is God and we must, with Jesus, bow down only to the God of our ancestors, the God of history, the God of life, the God of hope and the God of peace. So we need to come up with prayers – each of us, our families, our communities, the groups we belong to, our parishes and churches, our dioceses and universal religious bodies that ask us: 'What is your name?' For the Islamic community God has one hundred names, but only ninety-nine of them are known and the ninety-ninth and most powerful and descriptive name of God is 'Allah, the All Merciful'. Christians call God 'Father, Son and Spirit', a communion of intimacy and freedom where all belong and dwell as beloved children. For the Jewish people God is the God of life, the God of faithfulness and liberation from bondage, the God of the Sabbath and Exodus. And then we must pray, with each other, for one another, for our own conversion (not for that of others) and for the gifts of the Spirit of God that are dialogue, non-violent conflict negotiation, peace-making, wisdom and understanding of others and the determination never to do harm, certainly not in the name of our God. No matter what has happened to us or to those we love, no matter what we are afraid might happen, nothing is grounds for violent retaliation or extension. There is no 'eye for an eye or a tooth for a tooth' (and that's all that was ever mentioned – not a life for a life, or a rape for a rape, or torture for torture, etc.). There is only 'deliver us from evil [and from doing it ourselves]' and the clear-eyed, open-hearted and open-handed words of Jesus:

> But to you who hear I say, love your enemies, do good to those who hate you, bless those who curse you, pray for those who mistreat you. To the person who strikes you on one cheek, offer the other one as well, and from the person who takes your cloak, do not withhold even your tunic. Give to everyone who asks of you, and from the one who takes what is yours do not demand it back. Do to others as you would have them do to you. For if you love those who love you, what credit is that to you?... but rather, love your enemies and do good to them, and lend expecting nothing back; then your reward will be great and you will be the children of the Most High, for he himself is kind to the ungrateful and the wicked. Be merciful, just as (also) your Father is merciful.[4]

These words are central to Jesus' teaching. These are commandments as sure as 'thou shalt not kill', though we find them difficult. We must remember that these words of Jesus were uttered while he and all the early Church lived under military rule and were persecuted by the Romans, tortured to death, by crucifixion and in sadistic games in the arena where they were fed to wild animals and torn to shreds for entertainment or tied to stakes in the emperor's gardens, covered in pitch and set afire, to be 'the light of the world'. Jesus and the early Christians were not naïve or stupid – they sought to live in the freedom of the children of God, fear from their fears (they certainly had them, felt them and prayed for release from them and from what others did to them). They lived with the courage of the Spirit and refused to 'do unto others' the evil that was done unto them.

And these words were uttered by our Lord and Master who was betrayed by his own company of friends and followers, paid for with thirty pieces of silver, handed over by one of his inner circle, manhandled and slapped in a religious court of law that sought false witnesses to bolster a conviction of

4.   Lk 6:27-33 and 35-36.

blasphemy that warranted a death penalty. Jesus was deemed dangerous and a terrorist by the Romans (death by crucifixion wasn't for thievery but for seeking to undermine and overthrow Roman domination) and by some religious people intent on securing their place in a history that dominated them, but they had worked out a system of collusion, taxation and accommodation to an empire that still allowed them the outward rituals of worship, as long as they bowed down to the gods and idols of Rome that imprisoned them.

In Matthew's account of Jesus' life, death and resurrection the last time he is with his disciples and they hear him teaching, a mob comes with clubs and swords to arrest Jesus in the garden of Gethsemane. In the confusion Jesus stands calm in the midst of being kissed by Judas and handed over to guards sent from the elders and chief priests. Someone among Jesus' followers (traditionally it is Simon Peter) pulls out a sword that he has been concealing and cuts off the ear of the high priest's servant. Jesus, even though he is being dragged off by a mob, turns and commands, 'Put your sword back into its sheath, for all who take the sword will perish by the sword' (Mt 26:52). This is the last word of Jesus to his disciples, perhaps the most important word: direct, and in its context of violence, not something that can be easily rationalised or ignored.

Jesus is 'handed over' by Pilate to the praetorium guard, to a cohort of soldiers who tortured him as a game, humiliated him, mocked him and insulted not only his person but his belief in God. Abu Ghraib was where Arabs who practised their religion of Islam were tortured and humiliated in captivity by American soldiers. This was menant to instill fear in others. It is, sadly, a contemporary version of Jesus' torture – one among countless millions of such actions. This is the account we read usually only on Good Friday:

Then he released Barabbas to them, but after he had Jesus scourged, he handed him over to be crucified.
Then the soldiers of the governor took Jesus inside the praetorium and gathered the whole cohort around him.

They stripped off his clothes and threw a scarlet military cloak about him. Weaving a crown out of thorns, they placed it on his head, and a reed in his right hand. And kneeling before him, they mocked him, saying, 'Hail, King of the Jews!' They spat upon him and took the reed and kept striking him on the head. And when they had mocked him, they stripped him of the cloak, dressed him in his own clothes, and led him off to crucify him.[5]

Jesus and his followers were non-violent and courageous, seeking to live without doing harm to anyone, even to those who arrested them, accused them of terrorism against the state, heresy and blasphemy. This was the climate and the reality of the church for its first couple of hundred years when it remained faithful to the words and the living and dying of Jesus. Another victim of violence and torture, Sister Dianna Ortiz, OP, who was tortured brutally in Guatemala, wrote, 'At the core of the human spirit, there is a voice stronger than violence and fear'.[6]

There are still courageous free people who seek not only to speak the truth to a world in fear, but also stand in the freedom of the children of God in spite of torture, physical violence and what they have been subjected to while imprisoned. They even stand faithful to the heart of the Gospel and their own heart rooted in the heart of God in the midst of their church. By their very presence they say, 'No, I beg to differ. I will not live in fear nor will I react with violence'.

Another person who was quoted on the website is the writer, essayist and novelist Barbara Kingslover. She wrote: 'This is no time for naiveté. The writing has been on the wall

---

5. Mt 27:26-31.
6. Her story can be found in her book *The Blindfold's Eyes: My Journey from Torture to Truth*, Sr Dianna Ortiz with Patricia Davis, Orbis Books, 2002.

for some years now, but we are a nation illiterate in the language of the wall.' But, she says: 'We do what we can.' In one of her early books, *Animal Dreams*, there is a segment that one sister reads from another sister's letter, from Central America in the eighties:

> Codi, here's what I've decided: the very least you can do is to figure out what you hope for. And the most you can do is live inside that hope. Not admire it from a distance but live right in it, under its roof. What I want is so simple I almost can't say it: elementary kindness. Enough to eat, enough to go around. The possibility that kids might one day grow up to be neither destroyers nor the destroyed. That's about it. Right now I'm living in that hope, running down its hallway and touching the wall on both sides.

This is the second ingredient that is essential in combating war and violence, massive hate and destruction: she calls it 'elementary kindness'. Perhaps another term for it is universal justice. Enough of all the basic necessities of life, not just for survival day to day, but for sustenance and a bit of celebration that declares we are human beings and that we live humanly. It is not until all human beings are treated with respect and dignity and afforded what so many in the first world take for granted – the basic necessities of life and justice for all, that there will be security. If we are to look beyond our immediate fears and our usual reactions that are violence-based and violence-laced then we must look to the sacred obligation of justice. The only arms we are allowed to pick up are those against poverty and human misery and those arms are the physical arms of people helping others to claim their rights and dignity. The only sword we are allowed to grasp is the 'double-edged sword' of the Word of God that we use only on ourselves and never on another. Arms are for hugging, for embracing and for putting on one another's shoulders so that we can all dance together – they are not for killing and maiming or harming others.

In an interview with Laurens Van Der Post called 'Resurgence'[7] he talks about the Bushmen. What struck him almost forcibly was a statement one of them made when he was asking them about the fact that they were committed to no violence and that although they had their faults like any other people, they sought to balance their daily lives, with nature around them and a larger vision of the whole world. One man said: 'We did have one war and it was horrible – one man was killed.' Just one dead and that was enough. But Van der Post continued:

> One man was killed. That was enough. One man. It didn't have to be numbers. In this terrible world in which we live today, we think things only matter if we know them in numbers. We talk about the sum of human misery. There is no such thing in the wilderness. The sum of human misery is really an abstraction, because human misery is never more than what one person can feel. It is inflicted on one person at a time. This misery was enough for them. And I asked, 'What did you do?' They said, 'Well, we decided that those of us who had done the killing should never meet again because we were not fit to meet one another.'[8]

These are wise people, strong and courageous people. They call themselves the first people and they have learned what they must do in order to survive. When will we who call ourselves Christian (or Jewish or Arab or Muslim or American or anyone) learn?

I close with an Arab story called 'The Sword of Asharaf' and it comes from the desert of the Middle East and the tradition of Islam. The word 'asharaf' means 'noble' – so a literal translation is 'The Noble Sword'.

7. Appeared in *Utne Reader*, Feb/March 1985, pp. 122–6.
8. Ibid., p. 124

Once upon a time there was a sword renowned in legend that would come out of the desert like the wind. It was said that whoever owned this sword and wielded it would win every contest and battle, and reign over all the tribes and lands of Islam. Of course, every sheik and warrior wanted that sword. It was said that first you had to find it, then grasp hold of it, hang onto it and win it as your own in mortal combat. Then it was yours to possess and use. They all sent people to find it, search out every possibility of where it might be hidden or who might have it unknowingly in their possession. For whoever had that sword had the desert and the homage of all its people. Whoever had that sword had power beyond anything ever seen before among the peoples.

And then one of the sheiks found it. He was careful to make sure it was the sword of Asharaf. He practised with it and got used to the feel and heft of it in his hand. Then he went to battle, but not before he sent word ahead to all the other tribes and leaders that he came for them with the Sword of Asharaf in his possession. They all banded together against him in fear, hoping that together they might stop him. But this sheik had no fear. He felt that he could not be defeated, that he was invincible and that his power was unassailable. He went out to fight and what happened was not what he or anyone else expected. He was killed early in the fighting – impaled on his own sword!

The leaders gathered around him. The sword was wedged firmly into his body and the look on his face was one of utter surprise, as though his last thought was a question – what? or how? The leaders all wondered – was it really the Sword of Asharaf? And if it was, was it only legend that this sword brought victory to the one who used it? Was it just a sword like any other? They were all hunched over the dead man. Slowly one of them pulled the sword out of his bloody body and wiped it on his cloak. It shone brightly in the sunlight, glinting fire, and in the light they saw words engraved in

Arabic filigree that were exquisitely beautiful. The inscription read: 'Never fight with the sword. It is only through justice and understanding that others will bond with you.' They looked at each other stunned and speechless. The man repeated the message of the sword aloud, over and over again and all passed it by word of mouth to everyone gathered on the battlefield. They decided that day that it was the Sword of Asharaf, the most noble sword, and its words were truth.

In reality, only justice and understanding made you invincible and bound you in unbreakable bonds with others who became your allies, your friends and your family. While they had the sword, they refrained from violence, seeking the ways of peace and communion. But, it is said, they lost the sword. It is somewhere in the desert still, waiting for another to find it so that other kingdoms can be saved.

Our fear and obsession with violence, war, torture, killing and destroying other human beings proclaims that we worship these gods and bow down to them, waiting for such horror and terror to give us what we are afraid we will never have – power and security that is only ours. It is time to seize hold of the sword of truth, the sword of the Word of God and the sword of compassionate justice so that we might be saved from our fears and what the god of fear drives us to do.

Our God keeps saying to us: 'Take heart; it is I. Do not be afraid' (Mk 6:50). We are summoned to take hold of our hearts and to take hold of the heart of God and our God will abide with us, breathing courage, heart into us no matter what comes to pass.

Practice
Read Psalm 46 and reflect on 'the fearsome deeds' that God has done. What fearsome deeds would you like to be a part of doing with others. You might think of joining a group like Pax Christi USA or International and in public declare that along with God you are intent on 'stopping war to the ends of the

earth' and that you will vow not to live in fear. Write up your vow, or what you'd write on a 'sword' for all to grasp and wield.

4 SUFFERING, PAIN AND DISEASE

The soul grows by subtraction, not by addition.[1]

We begin with a children's story, a terrible one. It is terrible in its telling and in its truth. A version is one retold by Lee Oo Chung. This is the way I tell it. It is called 'The Emille Bell'.

Once upon a time there was a powerful king who was very devoted to Buddha and to his people. He sought to do everything he could to protect his people from invasion, pestilence, drought, famine and war. He lived in difficult times and his advisors counselled him to build a temple that could house a bell. The bell's tone had to be perfect – to sound far and wide; to be pure and lovely, summoning everyone to stillness and admiration. It was to be built to honour Buddha, who would in turn protect the people and the country. And so the king and all the people began their common task.

They laboured and constructed the buildings, but making the bell proved much more difficult. Every bell-maker in the land was invited to produce a bell of surpassing sound. They came with their bells: huge ones, tiny ones, ones that produced deep bellowing sounds that reverberated out, others that tinkled and chimed, but none was perfect – none was considered to be a pure sound. The temple was finished and still there was no bell. The king and the people were distressed – what good was the temple without the bell that would be

1. Meister Eckhart.

58

singular in its honour of the Buddha so that Buddha would protect them from harm, pain and suffering.

Finally the king summoned his advisors once again and the bell-makers. One of them, who had made many of the rejected bells, approached the king and told him there was a way to get a perfect bell but that it was terrible. The king demanded to know immediately. The man's answer stopped him dead. The only way to guarantee that the bell's sound would be pure and distinct from all others would be to sacrifice a girl child. The king barely hesitated: it was a necessary step to protect the country. He sent the soldiers to a distant village, with the order to seize a young girl child and bring her to the temple area. On the outskirts of the village they came across a mother and her young child on the way to the market, and grabbed the child away from her mother. The two of them screamed and cried out to each other. The little girl's piteous cries of 'Emille! Emille! Emille!' had no effect on the soldiers. They knew what they had been sent to do, and they would not question the king and his advisors.

Upon arrival at the temple, the bell-maker was ready. A huge vat was prepared of molten lead and iron. The temperature was white hot and at the right moment the young child was thrown into the vat screaming, 'Emille! Emille! Em...' and her voice and her life was silenced. They waited and then the liquid was poured out and the bell formed. It was hung and the first strike confirmed the old bell-maker's recipe – the tone was beyond description. Everyone stood transfixed. The sound was pure, strong, haunting and exquisite. They had finally succeeded in crafting a bell that was worthy of the Buddha.

The bell was called The Emille Bell, as was the temple that housed it. The bell was only used to summon the people to feast days or when something of import for the whole land was happening. And it was sounded with a great wooden clapper that was set in motion by one of the monks swinging it back and forth rhythmically on that one day, dedicated to the maker of the bell and all who were involved in its creation. People would stop in the fields, work suspended, and just stand and listen. They would stand in crowds together and listen to its tone carried on the wind. All would be amazed and praise those who made it, but also give themselves satisfied credit, as they too had been part of the endeavour to build the temple that would protect them.

But the mother of the young girl couldn't bear the sound of the bell. Every time it echoed across the fields and through the city streets, she covered her ears, silently screaming, and her heart broke yet again. She knew that her child had been sacrificed thoughtlessly and that the bell was evil to its core, except for the suffering of her child and her grief. And those who knew her and what had made the bell's power wept in pain. They stood and ached, their bodies and their minds torn by suffering that could not be expressed in words.

You see, only those who understand the loss, sacrifice and ugliness can feel the pain. Others just stand there and admire the sound. And the word Emille in the dialect of the region means: 'O Mother!'

The children's book has incredible art to accompany the story on the page. When I tell the story, I have a number of bells from the far East that I sound at various times, saving a specific bell for the ending. Our ears are connected to the deepest places of our psyche and soul, and people say it is the sound of the last bell that breaks them. They know it is only a children's story, but they also know it speaks hard truths about the pain, the suffering and the ache of being human and what human beings do to each other.

To be human is to suffer, to feel loss, for things to fall apart and unravel; for things to die and come to an end. There is all the horror humans do to one another, thoughtlessly, in rage and anger, or despair; in revenge; in greed and avarice; in situations of fear, rationalising why this is necessary. But there is also pain, suffering, sickness, aging and disease intertwined with grief and sorrow that is part of life. Irish poet Patrick Kavanagh wrote these words to describe ordinary life that is somehow bound to life that is universal, even bound to God:

> God is in the bits and pieces of Everyday –
> A kiss here and a laugh again, and sometimes tears,
> A pearl necklace round the neck of poverty.[2]

Oftentimes when I teach about death and loss, people tell me that they are not so much afraid of death (they say because they think they haven't been touched closely by it yet) but they are very afraid of suffering, of physical pain or torture, or the loss of their independence or abilities to see, hear, be mobile or know who they are and who the people around them are – these possibilities can make them even feel physically sick. They are not sure about how they would endure, be faithful or experience it without becoming bitter and selfish. They are afraid of what it would do to them, body, mind and soul. It is the sense that suffering and pain, especially if it is bound to grief or to any length of time, would be impossible to bear. Perhaps this is connected to the way we often relate to our bodies – as disconnected somehow from our souls. Old spiritualities often spoke of our souls being trapped in our bodies and that release in death would be a better thing. This dichotomy severs our feelings, our will (which is found in our heart in Middle Eastern and Asian belief) and our flesh, blood and bone from our souls, and so it can play on our minds, causing more suffering than the base of pain that is physical.

Suffering is all around us. If it does not make a home inside us, it is quickly found in our loved ones, family, co-workers or students. So many families are inter-generational because of age, healthcare costs and necessity. Parents are raising their children, but also tending to their own parents in the same house. Every one of us knows someone, often even someone

2. Patrick Kavanagh, *'The Great Hunger'*, Collected Poems, Allen Lane, 2007.

young, who has died from cancer or suffers from HIV-AIDS or Alzheimer's. It is not uncommon for people to know the experience of loss because of a drunk driver, an attack or many of the events that fill our daily news accounts. (If you watch the news diligently it might appear that everything out there is terrible and everyone is just waiting to prey upon anyone who just happens to be in the wrong place at the right time). How do we approach pain and suffering so that we do not gorge ourselves on the fear that precedes it and can accompany it? Abraham Joshua Heschel was reflecting on the long dying of a dear friend and wrote this while watching him suffer:

> The body is not a prison but an opportunity. We must distinguish between being human and human being. We are born human beings. What we must acquire is being human. Being human is the essential – the decisive – achievement of a human being.

I heard those lines more than forty years ago, standing in a packed classroom where Abraham Heschel was teaching. It is in my notes that were penned leaning my notebook on the back of the student standing in front of me, madly copying what was being said.

Perhaps another way of saying this and of dealing with the reality of suffering and pain in our lives is found in a Zen story told by the monk Eshin to his students. He said imagine that you are dreaming. You are being chased by a tiger. You know that it is a dream, but the terror, fear and anguish that you are experiencing is horribly real, almost tangible. You keep telling yourself over and over, 'Wake up! Wake up!' but it has no effect. The tiger is still chasing you and gaining on you every second. Here is your question: 'How can you wake yourself from your dream and all the pain and suffering it entails?' Answer: 'Stop running: Turn and embrace the tiger!'

This is not exactly the answer we might be looking for!

Turn and embrace the tiger – not only face the tiger, but embrace the tiger! But this exhortation, this wisdom is shared by many, including, it would seem, Jesus in the gospels.

There is a story told (this is from Mark's account, which is the more detailed) that is a story within a story, and we are watching it from the vantage point of those who are accompanying Jesus but not directly involved in what is happening until the very end. First a synagogue official comes to Jesus while he is in the midst of a huge crowd. His name is Jarius and he is desperate enough to debase himself and fall at Jesus' feet, pleading for his beloved daughter: 'My daughter is at the point of death. Please, come lay your hands on her that she may get well and live' (Mk 5:21-23). Jesus follows him immediately, with the crowd trailing along behind them, curious to see what Jesus will do. This is the essence of pain – the looming threat of losing a child, helplessness before sickness, death and love that makes one desperate. The story is interrupted because there are others, probably many others, in the crowd who are also desperate, who have suffered so long, and have been forced to suffer the indignity of illness along with the rejection and blame of others because they are sick – but out of the many only one moves. In her desperation, she will slow them down on the way to Jarius' house and his dying daughter.

> There was a woman afflicted with haemorrhages for twelve years. She had suffered greatly at the hands of many doctors and had spent all that she had. Yet she was not helped but only grew worse. She had heard about Jesus and came up behind him in the crowd and touched his cloak. She said, 'If I but touch his clothes, I shall be cured.' Immediately her flow of blood dried up. She felt in her body that she was healed of her affliction. Jesus, aware at once that power had gone out from him, turned around in the crowd and asked, 'Who has touched my clothes?'[3]

3. Mk 5:25-30.

We have heard the story, but perhaps it is in the details that we find solace, comfort and even strength. She has long endured pain, humiliation, the loss of her savings, fruitless procedures that haven't helped, but made her condition worse. And because it is a blood-related disease she is seen as 'unclean' religiously and so shunned, blamed and rejected. Somehow she has been made the underlying cause of her sickness; she is seen to deserve it because of something she has done or neglected to do. Her pain is multiplied by others' judgement, callousness and need to distance themselves from her and her condition.

She is desperate, intent only on touching Jesus' clothes. She has heard of Jesus and associates him with healing, with wholeness, with what is holy. And she wants to touch that power, to have that power seep through her body and know what it means to be healthy again. She has heard what Jesus preaches – about good news to the poor and lepers made clean and those imprisoned in their tombs, even their bodies released. Her ears are intimately bound to her heart and her hopes. She reaches out; she dares to touch him, breaking all the rules, for in her touch of him, he will be made as unclean and untouchable as she has been for so many years. She touches him with intent, to connect deeply with him, to touch his heart (will) and to know him. When we are sick, when we are severed from those around us, the need to touch and be touched is as strong as our need for water, food or survival.

Jesus knows he has been touched. In the midst of a pushing and shoving impersonal crowd of people there is someone who has sought his soul, his heart and spirit, to come into his presence through just his clothes. This is the essence of a healer, a physician, a doctor that knows the integration of body and soul. He turns to find out who it is that is reaching for him. This touch is where it begins. Those whom we refuse to touch, who we imprison and isolate in their own bodies, we condemn to a double death, of physical pain and spiritual desolation. Jesus turns to face her and to embrace her:

> And he looked around to see who had done it. The
> woman, realising what had happened to her, approached
> in fear and trembling. She fell down before Jesus and
> told him the whole truth. He said to her, 'Daughter, your
> faith has saved you. Go in peace and be cured of your
> affliction'.[4]

The connection is made. She responds to his word with her
words, pouring them out in 'fear and trembling'. This is fear
that is holy, life-giving, affirming and freeing, close to awe and
delight, tinged with an edge of mystery that always frightens
us. She tells him the whole truth – what was that like in
public? What was the whole truth – the long years of pain
suffered alone, being blamed, shamed, shunted aside, not
allowed to live with others, humiliated, taken by those who
sought her money rather than her health, battling for her own
mind, struggling to stay human and not let others maim her
spirit along with the havoc that disease was wreaking on her
body? Or was it the whole truth about longing to be touched,
to be held, embraced and loved, cared for by anyone, stranger
or friend, and what it was like to live accused by others' words,
silence and actions as though she was judged and sentenced
for twelve long years? Jesus' response is affirmation,
acceptance and praise along with the greeting and the
command of his own life: 'Go in peace, daughter, your faith has
saved you.' The initial and faithful response to pain must be
peace; expressed in words, in public, in acknowledgement of
the person, in allowing others to touch us physically and
deeply within our souls. The first medicine must always be
praise of the person, in their need and in their knowledge of
what makes someone truly human.

This is the story inside the other story that seems to have
been interrupted. While Jesus stopped to attend to the
unnamed woman, Jarius' child died. The delay was deadly.
Messengers have come with the news and with advice – don't

4. Mk 5:32-34.

trouble the teacher any longer. They, it appears, don't share Jarius' desperation or see his reaching out to Jesus in public as wise. Jesus' reaction is sharp and immediate: 'Do not be afraid: just have faith.' In other translations it reads: 'Fear is useless: you must have faith.' This is a unique assessment of fear – it is useless. It does not help in many situations – in fact it makes matters worse. What is needed, what is essential, is faith. What is faith? Some writings tell us 'faith is the substance of things hoped for' ... philosophical, but not necessarily something that we can grasp hold of when we are looking for a life jacket, raft or rope. Here's the dictionary's offering:

> **FAITH:** noun 1. complete trust or confidence. 2. firm belief, esp. without logical proof. 3 a. system of religious belief; b. belief in religious doctrines 4. duty or commitment to fulfill a trust, promise, etc. allegiance.
>
> 2. certainty, conviction ... other meanings: loyal, true, devoted, constant, resolute, reliable, close, exact, precise, perfect. Literal meaning: valid.

Again, not particularly helpful, except that faith is relational and expressed not necessarily in words, creed or verbal assent, but incarnated, enfleshed in another person. It is of long-suffering, enduring and of a deep nature, with the sense that nothing breaks its hold, however strained it might be or difficult to hang on. My Nana used to say: 'It's a great life if you don't weaken, dearie! Hang on for a dear life and then hang on for a dearer life!' That, in a sense, is faith. Or as a card I've seen says: 'If you've reached the end of your rope, tie it in a knot and hang on some more – besides the rope is shorter and you're closer to what you want.' There is always an alternative to fear – faith or enduring grace, plain hard endurance, courage or long suffering. There is always something.

Often just doing something creates what is needed. Jesus continues to Jarius' house and takes only Peter, James and John of his inner circle with him. They arrive there and the public mourning, keening and wailing has already started. Life outside goes on and the rituals of grieving, burial, getting on with life kick in quickly. Jesus rebukes them and he is shunned and ridiculed. There is always anger in the face of suffering that culminates in death because we feel so helpless. Anyone's death, whether it is someone we are close to or just familiar with, can be threatening and can call forth that anger. Anyone, like Jesus, who resists the usual cultic ways of dealing with or ignoring pain, suffering and grief can be the subject of that anger.

Jesus and the others walk past those who too glibly indulge in loud public mourning and they enter the house and the room of the child:

> He took the child by the hand and said to her, 'Talitha Koum,' which means, 'Little girl, I say to you, arise!' The girl, a child of twelve, arose immediately and walked around. [At that] they were utterly astounded. He gave strict orders that no one should know this and said that she should be given something to eat.[5]

We find out some interesting details: the young girl is twelve – as many years as the woman with the haemorrhage has been ill. The entire duration of her short life has been the time span of suffering and pain of the sick woman who has faith and has been saved. The young girl at twelve would have become an adult member of the Jewish community, committed to the covenant, achieveing the inclusion of the people in all areas of life, though she is still referred to as a young child so she has not yet celebrated this ritual of entering into the mature faith of the community.

Jesus immediately touches her, takes her by the hand. This is a phrase in Mark's gospel that is repeated often. It first

5. Mk 5: 41-43

appeared in chapter one, when upon leaving the synagogue and entering the house of Simon and Andrew, Jesus, upon being told about Peter's mother-in-law, 'goes to her, grasped her by the hand, and helped her up. Then the fever left her and she waited on them' (Mk1:29-31). In many ways the earlier story is like a mini-version of this longer story involving other people in a more public arena. Jesus' action is not only the tender regard for the child that the words 'take by the hand' describe but also a sense of power let loose and directed at her, found in the words 'grasped her by the hand, commanding her to rise!' She is being wrenched from sickness, suffering and death back into life. The word 'rise' is always connected to the belief in and faith of the resurrection of Jesus, and our own resurrections that begin in baptism to be fulfilled, we hope and enduringly believe, one day in fullness. Mark is echoing his larger faith in who Jesus is, found in the book of the prophet Isaiah:

> Here is my servant whom I uphold,
>> my chosen one with whom I am pleased.
> Upon whom I have put my spirit;
>> he shall bring forth justice to the nations,
> Not crying out, not shouting,
>> not making his voice heard in the street.
> A bruised reed he shall not break,
>> and a smouldering wick he shall not quench,
> Until he establishes justice on the earth,
>> the coastlands will wait for his teaching.

> Thus says God, the Lord,
>> who created the heavens and stretched them out,
>> who spreads out the earth with its crops
> Who gives breath to its people
>> and spirit to those who walk on it:
> I, the Lord, have called you for the victory of justice,

I have grasped you by the hand;
I formed you, and set you
    as a covenant of the people,
    a light for the nations,
To open the eyes of the blind,
    to bring out prisoners from confinement,
    and from the dungeon, those who live in darkness.[6]

This is what Jesus is doing. He is claiming the young girl for his way of living, his way of bearing suffering and pain, his way of reaching out for others, his way of grasping a person for the victory of justice in a world beset by darkness, imprisonment, physical lack, pain and illness. And the girl walks around, walks in the presence of Jesus and the community, and is fed for her life to come. In a primary sense this is baptism, eucharist and confirmation – initation into the community that grasps people in pain by the hand and claims them and their suffering for the victory of justice. This way of living humanly is found in tenderness, in consolation, in carefulness of anyone in pain, close to death, whether it is the death of the body or the flicker of hope in the mind and soul going out, in long illness or just the everyday bruises of living. This is having faith and turning from the uselessness of fear into the practice of healing, bringing hope, being with others as solace and touch, and resisting the forces of culture or society that just 'get on with life' in the face of suffering, death and grieving.

The woman in the crowd was desperate – oftentimes that is where faith and living with courage begins – and she risked breaking long-held laws that added to her pain, while allowing others to just ignore her suffering heart or excuse themselves from doing anything in the face of her sickness and suffering – even using moral grounds to blame her for her predicament – that of just being human and subject to all that life brings. Jesus praises the woman and uses her as a model for Jarius

6. Is 42:1-7.

and for all of us, saying – this is the way you live in pain and suffering, not letting fear paralyse you or keep you from embracing others. We are to turn and embrace the tiger! We are to turn and embrace all those who are suffering and in pain! We are to turn and embrace our own suffering and pain!

A doctor, a woman of wisdom named Rachel Naomi Remen, has written a book called *My Grandfather's Blessings*. She is a physician and a healer in the more ancient sense of making holy and whole those who are in pain, those around them and those who attend to them in their sufferings. In it she writes:

> We avoid suffering only at the great cost of distancing ourselves from life. In order to live fully we may need to look deeply and respectfully at our own suffering and at the suffering of others. In the depths of every wound we have survived is the strength we need to live. The wisdom our wounds can offer us is a place of refuge. Finding this is not for the faint of heart. But then, neither is life.[7]

We cannot escape dying. We cannot escape physical degeneration and illness. We cannot escape the pain of living. We cannot escape the suffering that others will inflict on us. But we can resist letting any of these realities make us less than human. When we are sick, we are not our illness. When we break bones or get older, we are not broken or decrepit. Even when we begin to forget and our minds drift, we are not our lacks and pains. 'The soul grows by subtraction, not by addition.' Meister Eckhart's line is true. But our minds and hearts and bodies too grow by subtraction, not only or necessarily by addition. The way to live truly is not in spite of the pain and sorrow that is part of living but by embracing them, by embracing one another and holding one another dear, by honouring and respecting both our own bodies and those

---

7. *My Grandfather's Blessings: Stories of Strength, Refuge and Belonging*, Rachel Naomi Remen, M.D., Penguin Putnam, Inc., 2000, p. 138.

persons we are given to touch, to affirm and be present to, to attend to in their sorrow and pain. The old adage of pain being doubled when you have no one to share it with is true and its other half is truer still: having others who will touch and embrace you and be present, listening to you and being with you in your pain makes it not only bearable, but can transform it, mutate it into a depth of awareness and even a gift shared intimately. Perhaps what makes us truly human is how much of others' pain we can share and hold, and by so doing we invite others to life ever more graceful and enduring.

We cannot obliterate the pain and we cannot let suffering dehumanise us. We cannot ignore our own and others' incapacities, weaknesses and debilities, and we cannot let anyone define a person by what happens to their bodies or their minds. Sometimes we cannot stop the pain but we can always stand there, with others, touching them, grasping them by the hand for the victory of justice, humanness and being beloved through it all.

There is a Jewish story sometimes told in the synagogue on the afternoon of Yom Kippur Eve that tells us how intimately we are all bound in life, and so in suffering and pain, in death and joy, and in all things.

Once upon a time all the children of Reb Yaakov Yisrael of Krements would go and visit their father on the eve of Yom Kippur to ask for his blessing. They tried to come together, but that was not always possible. One year, one of his daughters was busy with the children and the day lengthened and she realised that she didn't have time to stop by her father's house. Instead she grabbed the youngest of the children, leaving the eldest in charge, went to the synagogue and waited for him at the door so that she would catch him on his way into the service. The baby was fussing and she rocked him and cradled him close.

The rabbi, her father, arrived a few minutes early and found them at the door, off to the side, and both of them were crying. The rabbi looked at his grandchild, bent low and whispered, 'Little one, why are you crying?' To his surprise he answered, 'Mama is crying so I'm crying too'. The rabbi looked at his daughter, whose tears were streaming down her face. After a long, loving look, she said, 'Papa, I was so afraid that I would miss you and not get your blessings, your touch this year'. He gathered them both in his arms, embracing them tightly, and he cried too and gave them his blessing.

She slipped into the back of the synagogue with the child, now stilled and quiet, and the rabbi went immediately up to the front of the synagogue and started the service. He turned around with the tears still in his eyes, standing by the Holy Ark that held the scrolls of the Torah, and told everyone what had just happened. He began saying, 'If a young child cries because his mother cries, even if he doesn't know why she is crying, don't all of us have cause to weep too? For all of us know, deep in our hearts, that the Divine Presence, who has created us and calls us beloved and precious children [Book of Jeremiah], is weeping over all of us. It is written, "In hidden places my soul weeps." Look at the state we are in, all of us in this world – what we do to one another, what others do to us, how much we suffer. We must suffer as we must rejoice and enjoy life too, but so much suffering is not necessary. What are we doing to stop it? Who are we standing with? Who do we stand over protectively? Who are we weeping with?

'We have cause to weep! The Divine Presence is weeping over us. The Divine Presence is weeping for us and our pain. The Divine Presence is weeping with us.'

And as he spoke everyone in the synagogue began to weep together. It is said that their tears so moved them that they resolved to repent and turn to one another and to the Holy One with such passion that even Heaven wept and reached out to them.[8]

Pain and suffering are a mystery to engage with as well as endure, to be lived and cherished as well as anguished over.

---

8.   A version of this story is found in *A Treasury of Chassidic Tales: On the Festivals*, Rabbi Shlomo Yosef Zevin, Mesorah Publications Ltd, 1986, p. 102.

But they are richer and truer when shared with others, even if nothing can be done to stop the pain. Some ease comes with presence, with embrace and with grasping the tiger together. Fear is useless; keeping faith together, holding onto each other – this is what is needed.

Practice
Look at the rabbi's questions in the story and answer them for yourself. Which sufferings are necessary? Which are not? Who do you stand with and bend over protectively, touching them in their suffering? If you were ill, who would you want there – presence, words, touch? Pick a form of unnecessary pain, e.g. the lack of health insurance and healthcare for so many, and look at what you can do to make sure that everyone gets one of the basic rights of justice in their lives – medicine and care, clean water, food and shelter. Embrace the tiger with others.

5 THE FEAR OF ISOLATION, LONELINESS AND DESPAIR

Eyes can see anything but themselves.[1]

Most of us live in fear. Usually it's a low grade sort of fear that just is there underneath daily life and it rises in reaction to what happens around us. Sometimes it's an undercurrent that surfaces with changes in the weather, shifts of seasons or around the time of holidays. It can come out of nowhere, perhaps when watching other people, and we suddenly realise we are lonely. There are so many ways to describe this dis-ease that seems to be part of our bones, our psyche and our very soul. There are many children's stories that tell of a time before we were born when an angel kissed us – that's the reason some of us have dimples, a cleft on our chin or birth marks. But the stories speak of an original wholeness or, in Zen, our original face before we were born. There is a memory deep seated in all of us that longs, aches and yearns for that original tenderness and intimacy, that sense of what we were created to be and so what we truly are and a sense that home is within us if we could only sink down deep enough. Sometimes we project our sense of incompleteness onto another person and say that we are looking for a soul-mate, a soul-friend. But this sense of disconnectedness is a shadow that even those who are married and are faithful as friends and lovers can feel.

This inability to feel complete affects how we see ourselves

1. Serbo-Croatian saying.

and, of course, how we see others and how we think they see us. Our identity, our sense of self is not only restless, but it is insecure, fearful and threatened. We have myriad ways of reacting to this sense of being so ill at ease. We hide our vulnerability; we ignore it or seek to compensate for it with addictions to food, exercise, sleep, drugs, alcohol, shopping and so on. We look in self-help books for ways to control or repress our fears. Many of our fears dictate our lives, control our decisions and interfere in our relationships, work, study, even our religious devotions and moral choices. What we forget always is that we can't see ourselves clearly: we have blind spots; we are myopic and have stigmas that distort our perceptions in regard to ourselves.

Perhaps all these fears of inadequacy, emptiness, separation, isolation and not being loved enough by anyone can be connected to three roots: holes in our past, insecurity in the present and uncertainty about the future. We don't live in the present because we are burdened with the past and that distorts our futures. We live anxious lives. The philosophers call it existential angst; children refer to it as the monster under the bed waiting for us to let down our guard for even a minute. We remember so much of the past as only negative, as failure, as loss of control and all that followed as consequences, the harm others did to us, or what we think they did to us, and we nurse these wounds and slights. If our pasts contain traumatic events or violent experiences – either ones we experienced or ones that we did to ourselves or others, then that suffering seems to seep into every aspect of our lives and we live in varying levels of depression.

Someone once said that depression is fear turned inward upon ourselves and anger is fear turned outward onto others. We either beat up on ourselves or try to beat up on others. Not facing our past and acting consciously to be set free from its tentacles leads to most of our present fears: fear of commitment, love, trust, failure, rejection, loss, getting hurt;

fear of what others' think of us and living up to others' expectations; fear of God even and what may lie ahead – tomorrow and in the future. Not to face these old fears lets them continue to infect us and encourages them to dominate our lives. It leads not only to depression and a sense of isolation, but to despair and helplessness that can paralyse us so that we are no longer actually living. We might be surviving or on an endless treadmill or enduring a marathon that never ends. A number of spiritual writers and psychologists say that depression is the scourge and the plague of our societies today.

Some depression is a physical illness, sometimes connected with diet, exercise or lack of physical exertion, or chemical imbalances in the body and brain. These kinds of depression need to be dealt with medically. What we are looking at in this chapter is more what could be termed soul inertia, heart-hurt or spirit pain. These are part of the reality of what it means to be human in all its frailty and brokenness. They are part of the gift of living freely with the demands and responsibilities that come with daily being recreated or desecrated as individuals. Part of the process of living is dying and being revived – of healing, then falling down and getting up again, and again. Someone once sent me a card with a Zen saying: 'I fall down, I get up. I fall down, I get up. I fall down, I get up. And all the while, I keep dancing.' Our lives are rhythms and to stand still too long, especially inside in our minds, hearts and spirits makes us stagnant and open to decay. How does one deal with the past? James Joyce in *Ulysses* said: 'Mistakes are the portals of discovery.'[2]

Rabbi Harold S. Kushner, author of *When Bad Things Happen To Good People*, says: 'In the final analysis, the question of why bad things happen to good people transmutes itself into some very different questions, no longer asking why something happened, but asking how we will respond, what we intend to do now that it has happened.'[3]

How do we shift the weight of our lives from the past into

2. *Ulysses*, James Joyce, Penguin Classics, 2000.
3. *When Bad Things Happen To Good People*, Rabbi Harold S. Kushner, Anchor Books, Random House Inc., 1998, p. 124.

the present? The solution is that we forgive and, in so doing, untangle the coils around our hearts. A newscaster once told a simple direct story that must make us stop and decide what we are going to do – now. He said that he had been talking with Bill Clinton who had had an interview with Nelson Mandela less than two hours after he walked out of prison to freedom. He said to him: 'I know you say you are not bitter, but as you walked out of prison you must have hated the people who put you there.' Nelson Mandala replied: 'No, I did not hate them, because if I hated them they would still be controlling me. I'd still be in prison.'

If our fear of all that has gone before us can be transmuted into forgiveness, then freedom will come along with us as our companion. We begin by separating out the pain of what happened to us and the pain we have created with our reactions of guilt, anger, jealousy, resentment, frustration, loneliness or worthlessness. These are the emotional and mental additions to whatever we experienced. (One of the ancient Chinese sages said that if someone wants to give you a gift of any of these things, refuse the gift.) Then we need to roar like a tiger and let out everything that has been stored up inside us.

There is a story early in Mark's gospel called 'The Healing of the Paralytic'. Jesus is just beginning to journey from village to village teaching the heart of his message: 'This is the time of fulfilment. The Kingdom of God is close at hand. Repent, and believe in the Gospel' (Mk 1:14b-15). Repent! Relent! Release! Return! Rebound! Regroup! Regret! Reassess! Redeem! Repair! The kingdom of peace, of justice for all, of living in the freedom of the children of God is so close you can reach out and touch it, grasp hold of it – it's that close, one hand grabbing another hand.

Jesus is in Capernaum, sitting in a house with a number of scribes listening and watching – not so much to learn as to see if they can trip him up. The house is crowded and no one else can get in. We are told that Jesus was 'preaching the word to them'. But there is a group of people who have heard that he is in town and they are intent on getting to him – nothing will stop them:

> They came bringing to him a paralytic carried by four men. Unable to get near Jesus because of the crowd, they opened up the roof above him. After they had broken through, they let down the mat on which the paralytic was lying. When Jesus saw their faith, he said to the paralytic, 'Child, your sins are forgiven'. Now some of the scribes were sitting there asking themselves, 'Why does this man speak that way? He is blaspheming. Who but God alone can forgive sin?' Jesus immediately knew in his mind what they were thinking to themselves, so he said: 'Why are you thinking such things in your hearts? Which is easier, to say to the paralytic, "Your sins are forgiven", or to say, "Rise, pick up your mat and walk?" But that you may know that the Son of Man has authority to forgive sins on earth,' – he said to the paralytic, 'I say to you, rise, pick up your mat, and go home'. He rose, picked up his mat at once and went away in the sight of everyone. They were all astounded and glorified God, saying, 'We have never seen anything like this'.[4]

The man's friends are true. They break all the social mores of befriending someone who is sick and climb up on the roof, remove the tiles and lower the man down right in front of Jesus. Jesus looks up at them and, seeing their faith, friendship and compassion, is moved to pity for the man who cannot help himself. He calls him 'child' and forgives him. The good news is we are forgiven. Freedom is as close as reaching out to the hand that offers it and grasping hold. In Jesus, God does the reaching and grasps hold of each of us coming so

4. Mk 2:1-12.

close. It is others, the religious authorities, that are shocked. Jesus knows how people think and feel, and he turns on them, stopping them in their thoughts and revealing what's going on in their minds. A succinct question: what is easier – to forgive someone for whatever they have done and release them from the prison they inhabit in their own hearts (with the door locked firmly by other people who intend to keep them there) or command someone to get up and walk away, walk outside their prison into life?

The reality is that often it is harder to forgive than it is to break out of our prisons. It helps to have friends who will get us into position so that we can be forgiven and know ourselves as children and not as someone who has done wrong, made mistakes, stumbled all over our own feet. It's harder to be forgiven and take that reality as a lifeline than it is to remain inert. It is harder to forgive others, to allow them freedom and welcome into the present than it is to cling stubbornly to old beliefs, habits, attitudes and opinions of others, but it is as essential as air and water to the life of our spirits and hearts.

Jean Vanier founded the L'Arche Community in 1964 in France. It was then the first community that provided group homes for severely developmentally disabled people. Whenever he speaks to groups he begins by saying that we must remember who we actually are – that each of us is a child, frail and vulnerable, and this is our human condition. We must believe that we are loved, not because of anything we do, or what we possess, or because of our connections and power, but just because of what we are – 'we were born little and we will die little'. He refers to those who are depressed as those 'who are disabled by distress'. When he speaks about depression, about loneliness that debilitates he says it is an illness of the soul, of the energy, that blocks the spirit. We must look at ourselves, our poverty, our weaknesses and lack of strength and we must accept ourselves as we are, and truthfully try to accept others as they are.

All of us are seeking what we never had and are reluctant to look at who we truly are; all of us are in need of being healed and made whole and holy. It is our lifelong proposition and project, alone and with others. It begins oftentimes with forgiving others their humanity, accepting our own self and reaching out for the hands around us, both asking and receiving from others. Rachel Naomi Remen has written in her book what each of our healings might look like.[5]

> While an impulse towards wholeness is natural and exists in everyone, each of us heals in our own way. Some people heal because they have work to do. Others heal because they have been released from their work and the pressures and expectations that others place on them. Some people need music, others need silence, some need people around them, others heal alone. Many different things can activate and strengthen the force of life in us. For each of us there are conditions of healing that are as unique as a fingerprint.[6]

With the practice of forgiving, healing and turning into the present we look at other aspects of loneliness, insecurity and fear. There is a well-known Zen story that is a classic for forcing us at least for a moment to live totally in the present. Even our reaction to the story reveals to us where our tendency to dwell lies.

Once upon a time a man was crossing a field and noticed that a tiger was following him. The man began to run, with the tiger pacing him from behind. He was weakening, but the tiger kept steady. He was sure he could feel the tiger's breath on his neck. His fear gave him a rush and helped him keep running. Suddenly he realised he'd reached the end of the field – and the edge of a cliff. He turned to face the tiger, which was staring at him. He turned back towards the cliff edge and noticed a strong vine deeply rooted in the ground. Instinctively he

---

5. *Kitchen Table Wisdom: Stories that Heal*, Rachel Naomi Remen, Riverhead Books, 1996.
6. *From Spirituality and Practice: Living Spiritual Teachers Project: Rachel Naomi Remen*, Frederic and Mary Ann Brussat at *www.spiritualityandpractice.com*.

lunged, grabbed hold of the vine and began to lower himself down the side of the cliff. The tiger came to the edge and watched him, roaring. The man was grateful that the vine was holding his weight. But then he looked down and shook with fear. Below him was another tiger, looking up at him, pacing back and forth and waiting for him to fall. He tried to calm himself. He dug toeholds in the cliff face and decided to try to out-wait both tigers. Then he heard a scratching sound close to his face and dust began falling into his eyes – a couple of mice were gnawing away on his vine! The man's terror returned. Just then he noticed within arm's reach a huge deep-red strawberry, ripe and luscious. He reached out, took it in his fingers and ate it slowly, tasting its sweetness and tartness, licking the juice from his fingers. It was the sweetest taste of his whole life.

That's it! And perhaps that's life, right now, right here. Living life takes courage every moment, but oh the delights as well as the quandaries that are intensely a part of that living. When I tell this story so many people get frustrated – they want an ending – now! They want an answer – what happens? Some get angry and can even articulate that they feel caught, trapped between a rock and a hard place, with options running out. Others laugh and some even cry. Most say they don't like the story because it makes them get in touch with the general insecurity they feel about life much of the time.

How do we deal with the feeling of insecurity – of hanging somewhere between there and the unknown? How do we live in the present moment with courage or, as it is sometimes called, enduring grace? The emphasis is on a small detail – the verbs ending in 'ing': 'hanging', 'reaching', 'seeing'. All these things are ongoing in our lives, never completely settled or over and done with. This story is about an attitude, a way of life, that has been, is and needs to be until forever. Hope lies in the grace – actual, right now, every moment and perpetual or sanctifying – a state of being in grace, not in relation to sin, but in relation to living in grace, suspended in the Spirit, enfolded in the arms of the Holy, come what may.

Most of us don't think of ourselves as courageous and, frankly, we don't want to be. We'd rather take shelter from life, hide from the storm and set up shop, keeping things nicely under control. Listen to this remarkable description of how most of us either live our lives or often want to:

> A discarded bottle lying on the ocean bottom is, it seems, an irresistible temptation for a baby crab. The little creature glides easily through the bottle's mouth to discover an enclosed world that offers everything it needs: plenty of organic debris to eat, shelter from the strong currents and, best of all, protection from the countless predators who feed on young crabs. Delighted, it makes itself at home, and begins to thrive in the cosy surroundings. After some weeks, however, when instinct tells it the time has come to migrate, it crawls confidently to the opening, expecting to swim back out the way it came in. That's when it discovers the ghastly price of that time of perfect security: it has grown too big to fit through the neck of the bottle! In a terrible ironic twist, that safe shelter now becomes a death chamber; its protective shield will be its coffin.[7]

When this is read, the groans are audible. We recognise the situation described, but that doesn't keep us from trying to set up our lives this way. We might be crabs, but we are hermit crabs (a kind of crab that must break its shell as it matures) and we must shed our own encrusted shields and grow into something that gives us more space to expand. This is not about buying a larger house, but living so that we have larger hearts, minds and souls. A religious word for this is conversion: to keep turning, moving, shifting base and perspective; to keep breathing; dancing; learning and praying

---

7. Albert Holtz, OSB, in *The Monastic Way: Ancient Wisdom for Contemporary Living: A Book of Daily Readings*, ed. Hannah Ward and Jennifer Wild, Canterbury Press, 2006, p. 14.

– facing the tiger, facing the truth. It can be described as vigilance, of being awake, of making sure you're still alive! Albert Schweitzer wrote about it this way:

> You know of the disease called 'sleeping sickness'. There also exists a sleeping sickness of the soul. Its most dangerous aspect is that one is unaware of its coming. That is why you have to be careful. As soon as you notice the slightest sign of indifference, the moment you become aware of the loss of a certain seriousness, of longing, of enthusiasm and zest, take it as a warning. Your soul suffers if you live superficially.

Living in the present, facing reality is far richer and, in most instances, easier than living in the past. It is truer than living in fear of the future, or sliding into a fantasy world of our creation, or trying to collect things that will make us feel like we have a hold of our lives. We must begin by looking at what is happening in our lives and listening to what people are saying and to what that elicits in our own feelings and soul.

In the gospels Jesus is trying to do this all the time and his disciples are equally intent on ignoring what he's saying, especially with regard to anything they perceive as suffering or rejection, or as threatening their version of what they want reality to be – what they want Jesus to be and what they want their lives to be. It begins usually about half way through the gospel when Jesus asks them who other people say he is and then wants to know who they think he is. He gets a medley of answers: a prophet, John the Baptist returning, someone like Jeremiah. Simon Peter's answer is 'the Messiah'. Jesus shocks them and us by saying, in response to Peter, don't say anything like that to anyone. In essence he's saying, you don't know who I am and your ideas of what you want me to be are making my life more difficult and confusing others. The Scriptures say 'he begins to teach them', and what he has to say about who he is and what's going to happen to him if he keeps telling the truth, embracing others and seeking out the lost is not what they want to hear. In Mark it is most acute. He begins bluntly:

> He began to teach them that the Son of Man must suffer greatly and be rejected by the elders, the chief priests and the scribes, and be killed, and rise after three days. He spoke all this openly. Then Peter took him aside and began to rebuke him. At this he turned around and, looking at his disciples, rebuked Peter and said, 'Get behind me, Satan. You are thinking not as God does, but as human beings do'.[8]

Jesus is trying reality therapy on his friends and they don't want any part of it. The interchange between them is devastating and yet there is a shred of comfort there. Peter is thinking as human beings do – we all do. We want life to be 'nice'. We want life to be easy. We don't want to face rejection, suffering, pain or death. But there is something else underlying this encounter. Jesus knows what's going on around him. He knows the human heart and he knows his own heart. He has struggled long and hard to be honest with himself and to be truthful about what he will and will not do. And he wants his friends to stay with him, come what may. Peter and the other disciples, and every one of us, reacts with rejection of the reality, lashing out in anger at the person who tells us that life is hard. However, we must remember that life is also glorious and that Jesus rose again.

When Jesus tells the crowd immediately after this episode that living truthfully, living with integrity and honouring one's own soul are more important than anything else, we are told that 'they are deeply disturbed, distressed'. Specifically, he says that if we want to come after him we have to deny ourselves, take up our cross and follow him. We must deny our false selves – what others want us to be because it suits them.

8. Mk 8:31-33.

We must take up all of life, the bitter and the sweet, the hard and the fluid, the good and the bad, and we must live as fully as we can. We must follow what is the only way, the deepest truth and the most abundant life – watching every moment how Jesus lives as a human being and so as God among us. He continues:

> For whoever wishes to save his life will lose it, but whoever loses his life for my sake and the sake of the gospel will save it. What profit is there for one to gain the whole world and forfeit his life? What would one give in exchange for his life?[9]

What Jesus is saying is basic life-coaching. We are to live passionately with every fibre of our being, remembering that life is not primarily for ourselves and what we can get out of it, but with others and for others. Whatever serves abundant life for all, whatever serves hope and grace being together, that is the only profit that matters. What would any of us give in exchange for our lives? We are invited, as Jesus invites his friends, to live with him. They, in their fear, cannot respond. He tries again. He continues teaching, telling them what was going to happen to him – that his words and his life would trigger powerful responses both of passion that destroys and passion that loves. 'But they did not understand the saying, and they were afraid to question him' (Mk 9:30-32). They are afraid, but they won't say anything. A third time as he is walking on the road to Jerusalem, the city that is described as the place where the prophets (those who tell the truth about present realities) are killed, he tries again. This time 'they are amazed [the larger crowd with them] and those who followed were afraid' (Mk 10:32).

To live in the present, to dwell in grace, takes courage and a few friends. There will be light and dark places. Opposites attract and the extremes of both sides of reality are life. There

9. Mk 8:35-37.

is an extremely short Sufi parable that throws us into reality and gives another side to this being chased by a tiger.

Once upon a time a woman was being chased by a tiger. She was exhausted and could run no more. She stopped and turned on the tiger, crying: 'Why don't you leave me alone?' The tiger replied: 'Why don't you stop being so appetising?' We are alive. Are we appetising? We are so much more than we want to admit! The world outside us has everything to do with us and paradoxically nothing to do with us at all!

There is a story told of a pianist, Walter Nowick, who was playing Beethoven's piano Sonata no. 32, a composition noted for its difficulty. It was night and all of a sudden, in the middle of the performance, the power went out and the entire auditorium was plunged into darkness. Nowick played through to the end. Afterwards everyone wanted to know how he had managed to continue playing when he didn't have his sheet music to read. His reply: 'If you can't play it in the darkness, you can't play it in the light.' What keeps us playing is love. It can be love of music, of words, of science, of the earth, of someone, of friends, of God or of life itself, but it is love, infinitely bound to gratitude for life, raw life and all that is attached to living.

It is living that makes the future. It is living that makes the dreaming come true. We actually 'remember the future' in the sense of putting it back together the way it could be and was meant to be. To remember life; to remember each other; to remember everyone; to remember earth; to remember the Holy among us – that is how the future comes to us. Whatever the future is lies buried in seed already now in the present. It is found in our spirits, our hopes and dreams, and our will to live. Paul writes to Timothy what we need to remember and to share with others:

> For this reason, I remind you to stir into flame the gift of God that you have through the imposition of my hands.

> For God did not give us a spirit of cowardice but rather of power and love and self-control.[10]

Our spirits are strong, loving and wise. And we live, stirring that spirit in one another and letting others touch us so that we can express this spirit. Life is contagious and easily passed on to others. To face the fears of loneliness we need the antidote of solitude – time for our souls; for depression we need the antidote of the truth; and for isolation we need the antidote of reaching out to others. (The remaining chapters will look at some ways to take these remedies to heart.)

Loneliness, depression, isolation and discouragement do not have to lead to anger, fear or a diminished life. Those strong feelings can also lead us to the deepest places within where we sit face to face with ourselves and with The Truth. These feelings can lead us to transformation and power that jump-starts life, and provides a current of energy that is life-affirming and regenerative.

Now, a story which may offer a way to slip under the loneliness and despair of the life that often lies just under the surface.

Once upon a time there was a monk who daily would go to the edge of the jungle just as night would fall. She lived in India in a place that was the home of wild tigers. There were times when a tiger, looking for food, would come into villages, terrifying everyone. This monk had her daily ritual. She would gather herself and sit for most of the night, eyes closed, stilling her soul. She would pray, remembering everyone in the village, all the earth and its creatures and the world beyond the fields, into the wilds and past all borders and boundaries. She would send compassion and hope for an abundant life out towards each thing. As the sun rose, she would rise. One night as she was praying a stray kitten stumbled over her knees and then curled up and slept. When she opened her eyes the next morning she realised that many of the villagers stood waiting

10. II Tim 1:6-7.

for her to rise. They spoke with terror in their voices: venerable one, last night a man-eating tiger preyed upon the village. It doesn't seem to have attacked anyone, but the tracks are everywhere. And we have followed the tracks and they lead right here – to you! Have you seen the tiger?

She answered, 'If you plan on hunting this tiger and killing it, then no, I haven't seen the tiger. If, however, you just want to chase the tiger from your village and let him live in his place, then yes, I have seen the tiger. In fact, the tiger stands behind me even as we speak.' And with that the tiger roared! The villagers bolted and ran in terror screaming. And standing behind them, stood the kitten. The monk spoke: 'Ah, my venerable companion of the night, I pray you find food in the jungle and do not have to come looking in the village. But if you can't, I will be here every night and you are welcome to come and sit with me.' And the tiger bowed and slipped away into the jungle.

Many tigers recognise their own kin when we stay still long enough to face our tigers, all the time grasping hold of the strawberries growing so close to us. Some tigers befriend us, as kittens purring and curling up beside us and others as tigers standing behind us, roaring when it is necessary.

Practice

This is a prayer for today and every day. It is by Saint Teresa Benedicta of the Cross (1891–1942) who was born Edith Stein, a German Jew, philosopher and writer who converted, became a Carmelite and died in the Holocaust. Her feast day is 9 August (also the day of the bombing of Nagasaki, Japan).

> O my God, fill my soul with holy joy, courage and the strength to serve you.
> Enkindle your love in me and then walk with me along the next stretch of road before me. I do not see very far ahead, but when I have arrived where the horizon

now closes down, a new prospect will open before me, and I shall meet it with peace. Amen.

6 MONEY, POSSESIONS, INSECURITY

Ah, but you must also understand 'and'.[1]

The fear of the future is often pragmatically connected to the fear of not having enough, of financial insecurity and the fear of losing one's independence and not being in control. Money, 'filthy lucre', bread, mammon, coin of the land, currency, medium of exchange, wealth, cash, loot, dough, bucks, riches, the root of all evil; resources, finances, capital, fortune, funds. The ways of describing money seem endless. In the United States the currency all reads, 'In God we trust', and so is often the source of many double entendres about what actually is the god of the country.

For many people one of the most troubling fears is that of money. With the fluctuating markets and economies of the world, will they have enough? Will their money hold out as long as they live? Will they be able to live in the style they have grown accustomed to or will they have to radically alter their lifestyles just to have the necessities?

Then there is the issue of 'what is enough?' Often, when people have more than enough, more than they need, they suddenly feel that they need still more. This is the question of the difference between what we need and what we want. This holds true even more in first world countries where the issues are often dealt with in a climate of advertisements, pressures to

1. Quote from Jelaluddin Rumi taken from *The Way of Wisdom*, Margaret Silf, Lion Hudson, 2006, p. 13.

spend and to keep the economy going (even as part of a war effort!), and a culture that prides itself on what it possesses, how much someone owns, what a person's net worth is and how to live in relation to others' concepts of rich, upper and lower middle class, poverty and human misery.

According to the United Nations, 'If you have more than what you need today, you are rich'. This statement reveals that the majority of the world looks at money, finances and sustenance in regard to daily needs, while a small portion of the world looks at the issues, not only for today, but for decades in the future, trying to cover all possibilities. While this definition of rich often causes stress in those who hear it, it is not that far removed from one of the primary phrases in the prayer of Christians, the Our Father – 'Give us this day our daily bread'. This phrase comes immediately after the petition 'Your kingdom come. Your will be done on earth as it is in heaven'. Somehow we often manage to disconnect the essential need for everyone's daily bread from the will of God for all on earth and that this is the first way God's kingdom comes to the earth. We also forget or ignore that all that is given is from God and all that we receive and take, we are to share with others so that God's will becomes the reality of earth. Rigoberta Menchu wrote in her autobiography, *I, Rigoberta: An Indian Woman in Guatamala,* these words that are theology at its truest and deepest:

> We feel it is the duty of Christians to create the kingdom of God on Earth among our brothers and sisters. This kingdom will exist only when we all have enough to eat, when our children, brothers and sisters, parents don't have to die from hunger and malnutrition. That will be the 'Glory,' a Kingdom for we who have never known it.[2]

---

2. Translated by Ann Wright, Verso, London, 1987.

It is interesting to note that in so many languages of the world, the word for money is almost synonymous with the word for bread. Money is for necessities, for the basics of life and what sustains human beings first. What is excess or extra belongs somehow to others if we are Christians. There is a remarkable story a Jewish rabbi shared with me about a man named Sir Moses Montefiore (1784–1885). He was a British financier and philanthropist. A man at a cocktail party once asked him what he was worth. Sir Moses replied: 'I am worth about £40,000.' 'Is that all?' was the shocked reaction. 'I thought you were worth millions – that's what the finance pages would have us believe.' Sir Moses said, 'In one regard you are absolutely correct. I do possess and have many millions of pounds at my disposal and for investment purposes. But you didn't ask me what I had – you asked me what I was worth. There is a enormous difference in the questions. You see, £40,000 was the amount of money I gave away and distributed to various institutions, charities and individuals in need in this past year. This is what I am truly worth. Since I was a child I have known that it is not how much a person possesses, especially when it comes to money that says what they are worth; but it is what they have shared with others in need that determines their actual net worth.'

Oh my! What if this is true? This understanding of money and what you do with it, and how it is to be viewed and used is shared by many Native Peoples. In many native communities one's status and respect is connected to what one shares and gives away to others. One ritual is called a 'Showing': on the anniversary of a person's death a tribe will invite everyone in the village to come to a feast, during which they tell stories of that person and then everyone goes home with food, blankets, baskets and gifts from the family. Many tribes have a give-away every year. Everyone brings something they have not used, do not like or have more than one of to the middle of the village. All the things given remain there for a few nights and everyone comes and takes what they want, having left things in their place. Possessions are for use and to circulate around the community as needed.

Someone once told me that a computer study had been done on the issues that Jesus speaks about in the four gospels and that surprisingly (or not) the topic that he speaks of most often is money. Luke's gospel is laced with stories of wealth and rich young men, of building barns to accommodate bigger harvests, strain in family relationships over inheritance, talents (the largest amount of money at the time) and what one does with them – invest them to varying degrees of return or bury them in fear.

The parables are many: the barn and the reckoning of its builder that very night; Dives (meaning rich man) and Lazarus, the man so poor at his gate that the dogs lick his sores and the reversal in the after-life told as a warning to change one's ways in this life; the vineyard owner who pays everyone the same daily wage, no matter how long or how short their period of work; and the dishonest steward who, when he's fired for embezzlement, goes back and 'cooks the books' so that his master's business partners will take him in and help him out, perhaps even give him employment because they will all be aware of how shrewd he is in fending for himself and his future.

Then there is the story of the rich young man who wants to know from Jesus what he needs to do to get into this kingdom that Jesus preaches about with such passion and insistence. He initially sees himself as jumping all the hurdles (the major commandments) and then Jesus looks at him with love and shocks him:

> Jesus, looking at him, loved him and said to him: 'You are lacking in one thing. Go, sell what you have, and give to the poor and you will have treasure in heaven; then come, follow me.' And at that statement his face fell, and he went away sad, for he had many possessions.[3]

3. Mk 10:21-23.

It seems, according to Jesus, that heaven is found among the poor and what we lay up in heaven is intimately connected to what we give away to the poor. The man is rich and so the one thing he is lacking is that he has no awareness that he is bound to others and that his excess contributes to the cause of suffering, hunger, no shelter, water, medicine, etc. among so many of those who we call 'the poor'. His wealth has distanced him from being human and the need to be compassionate. It truly is the one thing he lacks – for even Jesus' invitation to closer intimacy, friendship, a place in his inner circle of disciples isn't enough to remove his clutching hands from what he possesses. In fact, all his possessions have clutched at his heart and claimed his worship.

One of Jesus' rarely quoted lines is:

> No servant can serve two masters. He will either hate the one and love the other, or be devoted to one and despise the other. You cannot serve both God and mammon.[4]

This is a statement of reality, but that doesn't stop us from trying to juggle taking care of ourselves, collecting and gathering, living often beyond our means, getting in debt over luxury items or houses that come with dangling mortgages that we were sold in our desire for more. Our greed and our want say something about our lives to others, and to ourselves. The gospels are fraught with the tightrope walk of how to care for one's self and one's family's needs while also being aware of the larger community's needs. The rope is strung between the two poles of trusting in God and having bouts of fear connected to money, possessions, finances, the future and what we want.

I sometimes ask people to look at their chequebooks or statements online and put a column of where the most money goes. Apart from the basics – rent/mortgages, car payments, insurances, food, phone, education, transportation – what they

4. Lk 16:12-13.

do with the rest of their money. This exercise and the statement 'Anything you write off your income tax isn't charity' does not sit well with most groups. We are all intent on securing our own welfare, taking care of ourselves and securing our futures while at the same time reacting in a number of different ways religiously. We can say that we trust God, but God takes care of those who take care of themselves. We can say that economics, finances, lifestyles of excess don't have anything to do with religion (along with politics, and the majority of the human race and other areas of life). We can say that we give our excess to our families and so excuse ourselves from living beyond our blood or marriage ties, allowing ourselves to ignore those who are poor and in desperate need, who are not technically our family (this response ignores the fact that we are baptised and that in the Christian community water is thicker than blood. The only blood thicker than water is the blood of Christ found in the Eucharist and in those who suffer with the crucified Lord). Or we go to other extremes. We follow the religious groups that adhere to lines taken out of context in either the earlier or new testament and claim that riches and wealth are a gift of God that show that God loves us more than others and that no one else has any claim on our excess. Or another extreme that says we must trust in God for everything and do nothing, just wait for God to come through and take care of us, living selfishly as though it were God and us only in the world and that God has nothing better to do than take care of just us. We are strange creatures when it comes to money and the number of ways we avoid looking at what Jesus actually says about money, about the poor and about sharing is hundred-fold!

Jesus has much to say to us in regard to working for what we need while remembering that we are to work for the coming of God's ways and kingdom and economies in the world. Our households must reflect God's values, God's presence and God's economics. This way of God is an intertwining braid of trust in God, sharing with others and living from a standpoint of gratitude. Chapter 12 of Luke is all about money, possessions, riches, greed, servants and masters, and how to live with our eyes fixed on the larger vision of God's hopes for the earth and all the children of God. Strewn throughout is the recurring phrase: 'Do not be afraid. Fear not little flock.' Along with the exhortations against fear are commandments about courage and standing fast in the face of others who will persecute you, take advantage of you and seek to harm you. Throughout this chapter, Jesus' teaching on money and necessities, greed and trust begins with a question from someone in the crowd. He wants Jesus to use his knowledge of the law in the areas of inheritance and money to shore up his own complaint against another member of his family. Jesus will have nothing of it – he will not allow anyone to use religion to decide issues the way the rest of the world does. Jesus is interested in all things, money and economics and law serving those who are the most in need – the poor. He is blunt about saying that this is God's position on all these matters as well. With the exchange back and forth he would have had the whole crowd's attention – these are issues everyone has a stake in.

> Someone in the crowd said to him: 'Teacher, tell my brother to share the inheritance with me.' He replied to him, 'Friend, who appointed me as your judge and arbitrator?' Then he said to the crowd, 'Take care to guard against all greed, for though one may be rich, one's life does not consist in possessions'.[5]

Most of us don't think of ourselves as greedy. Greed is one of the seven deadly sins, meaning that its practice is mortal. It destroys us at our roots and leads to other evils: avarice, violence, jealousy, pride, arrogance, aggressiveness, lies, treachery and oftentimes using religious tenets to validate what

5   Lk 12:13-15.

we are doing, in direct opposition to the true teachings of religion. In America there is a line on bumper-stickers and posters saying, 'Greed is good'. The pressure to keep spending money is relentless and hard not to succumb to. Greed and selfishness are bound like hand and glove.

The dictionary definition of greed is incredibly short: an excessive desire, usually for wealth or food; connected to voraciousness, gluttony, avariciousness, covetousness, materialism, and mercenary. It is the adjective 'greedy' that has almost an entire column of meanings. In the *Oxford American Desk Dictionary* it is specifically connected to Americans, though with the tag that not all Americans are greedy. And then it details specific characteristics of being greedy: insatiable desires for anything, gluttony in regards to food and drink, using the word consumption and implying harm to oneself and others. Then there is avariciousness only connected to money, and rapaciousness, which is an even stronger term, when greed leads to taking what one wants by force; and being acquisitive with the sense that one works to obtain what one wants, but overworks and concentrates on that desire to the detriment of all other things. Lastly there is covetousness – the wanting when one cannot actually acquire it. Jesus is clear – we are supposed to shun all forms of this behaviour, attitude, practice and desire, and what feeds it.

There is the word 'consumerism' – the economic drive and pressure to buy. The word base is, however, to consume or to be consumed by. Not so long ago, the word 'consumption' was tied to a disease: tuberculosis. When people were found to have the virus, they were removed from the general population and forced to rest, read and write (many great writers discovered their gifts in TB hospitals) and to get their strength and their health back. Now the word's meaning has been flipped; in many societies, to consume is a virtue to be practised assiduously, even as proof that you are behind the war effort to encourage an economy. Perhaps consumerism is still a disease that breaks the strength of human beings and separates them out from others, from sharing, from practising compassion and even being aware of anyone besides oneself and one's small circle of engagement.

Jesus tells a short parable about a man who has a great harvest, so much so that he can't store it, so he decides to tear down his old barns and build bigger and better ones to store his good fortune. Jesus' listeners would have known the situation just as we do today. They would know that Jesus was silently condemning the man because it was understood in the Jewish community that one was to share their good fortune with their own: the poor, the widow, the orphan and those whose fortunes were not as good. Jesus is telling the story in the midst of the Jewish nation living as slaves in their own land, occupied by the empire of Rome who took everything they could from them, including the harvests, to feed their armies. Jesus quickly brings the parable to a violent end. The man is a fool, for the very night that he decides to 'eat, drink and be merry' he is going to die – and then who will get all that he has amassed in his lifetime? The last line of the parable is: 'Thus will it be for the one who stores up treasure for himself but is not rich in what matters to God' (Lk 12:16-22). The parable is referred to as the rich fool, associating the two traits as bound together.

Jesus' teaching begins with the negative aspect – greed – and then continues onto how to live in the world gracefully. He turns to his disciples and teaches them to look around them, to see themselves in the context of the larger world, the universe, and to take to heart how the world is designed so that everything is in balance, in harmony and taken care of when we also play our part in that larger picture. His words are not just nice sentiments but foundational perspectives on how we are to deal with the creeping fear of making it in this world:

He said to the disciples, 'Therefore I tell you, do not worry about your life and what you eat, or about your body and what you will wear. For life is more than food and the body more than clothing. Notice the ravens: they do not sow or reap; they have neither storehouse nor barn, yet God feeds them. How much more important are you than birds! Can any of you by worrying add a moment to your life-span? If even the smallest things are beyond your control, why are you anxious about the rest? Notice how the flowers grow. They do not toil or spin. But I tell you, not even Solomon in all his splendour was dressed like one of them. If God so clothes the grass in the field that grows today and is thrown into the oven tomorrow, will he not much more provide for you, O you of little faith? As for you, do not seek what you are to eat and what you are to drink, and do not worry anymore. All the nations of the world seek for these things, and your Father knows that you need them. Instead, seek his kingdom, and these other things will be given you besides. Do not be afraid any longer, little flock, for your Father is pleased to give you the kingdom. Sell your belongings and give alms. Provide money bags for yourselves that do not wear out, an inexhaustible treasure in heaven that no thief can reach nor moth destroy. For where your treasure is, there also will your heart be.[6]

In this long paragraph is found gems of wisdom and suggestions for how to live without anxiety and worry, how to trust in God for what we need and how to live in a world that is in opposition to the values of sharing, justice, generosity, courage, community and trust in others along with trust in God. We must put ourselves, individually and in our primary relationships, in perspective with the rest of the world. We must start by looking out at the world – at the birds, ravens

6. Lk 12:22-34.

specifically, all manner of blackbirds, crows, grebels, sparrows rooks, etc. These birds are numberless and travel usually in large flocks. The image is of birds, not sheep! Most birds eat eight times their body weight every day just to survive – and yet they are taken care of, there is enough of what they need to survive in the world – and we are worth more than birds! The first principle of kingdom economics is *there is enough for all.*

Then we are bluntly told – get over yourself! or, as young people say often, give it a rest! Worrying, having anxiety attacks, thinking and fantasising about money and what we need or even what we want endlessly gets us absolutely nowhere, except perhaps it makes us ill, gives us headaches, upset stomachs, ulcers and who knows what else that breaks us down physically and emotionally. Beyond anxiety and worrying is catching sight of the beauty and the extravagance of the world – everything that is out there that is beyond what we need: flowers, the grasses of the field, all that exudes goodness and loveliness, scent and sight to ease us and add intangibles to our lives. We last a lot longer than most flowers and each of us is as treasured as these fleeting beauties all around us.

It is necessary to work for what we need, but we are not to be fixated on working to survive, working to get more and more or working to make a profit at the expense of others' lives. If we do, then we do not dwell in God's realm but we live tooth and claw, competitively intent on profits over the needs of the majority of people (a blunt description of rapacious capitalism). We are called to live an alternative that is life-giving, sharing and hope-filled. We must work for a universal justice for all, making sure that our primary focus and dream is that we serve the human family and share our excess generously with others. Our religion, what ties our lives together, is giving thanks by sharing with others all that has been shared with us.

We are 'a little flock' – we are bound together and we must see ourselves and our needs together. We are told boldly that if we think in terms of a larger dream, a larger family of humankind, a larger company of friends, then we will risk sharing by 'selling our belongings and giving alms' to those who are the living presence of God's dwelling place on earth – the poor. Whatever we share with them will be laid aside as our portion in God's place. So we must ask ourselves, does our fear reveal where our hearts are caught – in the grip of what we are told we need by a society that is intent on profit and inequality, that this item will make us more acceptable, likeable, included, more worthy to be a part of this country, this culture? Or do our lives reveal God's pleasure with us and that we already have God's kingdom with us now, here in this world and in our lives?

We absolutely need to be in relationships of sharing, of give and take and in communities where those who lack more than we do are honoured and included, never shamed, only sheltered and gifted. They in turn will gift us with gratitude, with a sense of love, compassion and freedom that can only come from being connected, by being responsible for others and being called beyond ourselves to generosity. Where are our hearts? Do our hearts beat stronger and surer among others? Do our hearts thrive in sharing, with reciprocity? Do our hearts thrill to be able to empty our storehouses and barns so that others can have what we don't need right now? Do our hearts race with the energy of the Spirit that is loosed in a community when we trust that there will be enough and act upon that trust? Do we remember in the deepest places of our hearts that God's word and the hearts of others can dispel our fears? Do we remember to tell others that 'God our Father knows that you need all these things' and that when we imitate God's graciousness to us by turning and being gracious to others, we can sense the very pleasure of God? This is fearlessness and courage when it comes to money.

We start by stopping the gathering, storing, collecting, acquiring, accruing and then we start selling off what is excess, what we don't need or use so that we can make sure that others have what they need. I saw a sign once outside a car boot sale that read: Someone's trash is someone's treasure! Our trash, our extra, our unused, is someone's treasure. In giving it away it becomes our treasure as well. Then we begin to treasure people more than possessions so that we can trust each other more than economics. A little risk goes a long way towards emptying us out so that we can know more of the fullness of life. How we look at money and what is given to us or what we work for beyond what we need reveals whether we are becoming 'good news to the poor', the 'light of the world' and 'a little flock that fears not!'

Indries Shah tells a story in his book *Learning How to Learn: Psychology and Spirit in the Sufi Way*[7], that uses animals – a fox, a tiger and others – that become sources of food to remind us of ways we can approach need, trust and sharing by looking at ourselves in relation to others and to God. This is how I tell it.

Once upon a time there was a hunter. He was the best in the village and always came back with more than his family could use. He shared the extra with the elderly, the sick, the young and those who did not fare as well when they hunted on some days. One day as he was setting out his traps and waiting, he saw a fox that was injured – it had lost two of its legs. Otherwise it looked healthy, even well-fed. He knew that foxes loved their freedom and he'd heard that a fox caught in a hunter's trap would sometimes even chew off a leg in order to get free. He decided to watch this fox and see how he survived in spite of the fact that he only had two legs.

He waited for hours and his wait was rewarded. He was shocked to see a tiger come into the clearing dragging what was left of a deer carcass. The tiger was wary and careful, but brought the leftovers and dropped them in front of the fox, who began to eat hungrily. The hunter was amazed – he'd

7.   The Octagon Press, 1966, p. 188.

never seen anything like this before. He spent days watching the fox and the almost daily visits of the tiger. The tiger always came with something to eat. Sometimes he ate first and left the rest for the fox and sometimes he just dropped part of his kill before the fox and left. The man was very religious and began to think to himself: God is great. God even feeds the fox by means of the tiger! How feeble my faith is – I work and work every day and I do not trust that God will take care of me and my family. So after thinking about it for a while he decided that instead of hunting he would trust God to feed him and take care of his family's needs.

Days passed and he did not go out to hunt. His family began to slowly starve and everyone else that he had helped began to grow faint and sickly. He himself was getting weaker by the day because no one brought him game or food – they were busy and intent on getting what they needed and often there was no extra to pass around. No one understood why he had stopped hunting – was he ill? But he said nothing. His wife pleaded with him; his children cried in hunger; but he kept reminding himself of the tiger that fed the fox and that obviously God was trying to teach him to trust that, like the fox, he too would be fed. He just had to wait and be patient and trust in God's providence.

One night he dreamed of the tiger bringing food to the fox just as he had seen it that first time and he was crouching in the bushes, hiding and watching in awe. This time he heard a voice speaking to him clear as a bell: 'O you fool! Why do you think that you're the fox? Open your eyes to the truth! You are the tiger! Go and make sure those who are hungry get fed.' And he woke up.

We are called to be the tiger while we are able and trust that if we are ever in the fox's predicament then there will be other tigers in our life. Besides what we do in regard to our money and our possessions, we must look around us and begin to practise the virtue of being hope for others and of crying out, calling out and singing the reality that there is enough for everyone's need. And there is more – more of beauty and more of extravagance, gifts and gestures that are treasures beyond compare, given to us to share as surely as justice, food and necessities. We could begin with John Muir's attitude when he described how he wanted to be in the world: 'I care to live only to entice people to look at nature's loveliness. My own special self is nothing. I want to be like a flake of grass through which light passes.'

We must learn to be doorways and windows of hope, courage and life with a future that is made of light and shadow, fullness and emptiness, gift and need, courage and a healthy fear of the hard work and trust that reality demands. We must decide and will that life is filled with imaginative creativity and possibility – this is belief in resurrection and life, and it is found, when you look, in the inexhaustible diversity of creation all around us. What comes forth from our mouths and is expressed in our gestures must be hope-filled. Writer Susan Chernak McElroy wrote an amazing piece in her book *Why Buffalo Dance: Animal and Wilderness Meditations through the Seasons*[8] that we must remember and repeat, each in our own inimitable ways:

> Hopelessness is like getting your skin wet and exposed in winter – all the heat leaches out of you, and the ice finds your heart, and that is that. But on solstice night, I heard the faint hooting of the owl. Even more than that, I heard the promise of renewal whispered in the tones of his call. Perhaps I heard him because I had lived through a half-century of winters, and my ears were open to a simple faith that winter ends and hope lives.
>
> Hope is not a gift we can sustain simply by our own will. Hope is something we need to hear from outside ourselves sometimes. Like the fire needs the help of a branch to grow its warmth, we need a voice sometimes,

8. New World Library, 2007.

or a sight, or visitor, to fan the flicker in our hearts when faith grows dim. On solstice, the voice came to me in the call of an owl, but nature has endless other voices that speak of hope: the sound of water to a thirsty creature, the breath of sunshine on a cold day, the call of kin and kind to one who is lost.

We are commanded to be children of hope, children that trust and children that watch all of creation to learn how to live without anxiety and fear, beyond living to work and survive and accumulate. We are asked to live in a way that is rich in giving and receiving in a rhythm that strings us all together and reminds us daily that we are the only treasure that gives great pleasure to God – and we do it by giving back and forth to each other.

Practice
Take an inventory of your excess as opposed to what you need and use. One formula: if you haven't used it in a year then it's excess or unnecessary and someone can either use it, or you can sell it to provide something that others need. Don't just do it yourself, or with your family, but gather with others and have a huge sale to benefit a specific group of people in need.

In celebration of your emptying out, do something extravagant for someone in need – not necessarily with money, but with something that will be an unexpected gift that will be treasured as an experience, a memory or something tangible, but not all that 'useful' except in the realm of beauty.

7 FEAR OF THE OTHER — THE STRANGER

THE IMMIGRANT, THE REFUGEE, THE ALIEN

> Be prepared for truth at all hours and in the most fantastic disguises. This is the only safety.[1]

'The other' covers multitudes of people, including anyone who is different to us, whom we perceive as separate or distant from us, either geographically or in culture, race, religion, language, way of living or expression of their value system. To use the word 'stranger' changes the equation, adding a note that has a strain of fear and a sense of uneasiness about it. Now all those people are not only other than us, they are unknown to us, new to us, unfamiliar to us. Words that we associate with a stranger can be 'foreigner', 'outsider', 'alien' and we tend to lump these people in groups of 'them' as opposed to 'us'. Yet the word 'strange' really doesn't have any of these negative connotations. The emphases in the dictionary definitions are on 'newness, surprising, unusual, peculiar, novel, intriguing, odd, curious, uncommon, exotic, unknown' – and only as a final description 'uneasy, uncomfortable or awkward'. The designation of another person as the other or the stranger basically reveals our position in relation to them but not anything of substance or depth about them. These masses of people reveal the astounding range of our fear of what is unknown.

For those steeped in a Judeo-Christian tradition the books of Exodus and Deuteronomy and the psalms are rife with

1. Christopher Morley.

reminders of having once been slaves and sojourners in the land of Egypt before God, who is a God of freedom, brought us out of that place. The Hebrew word for Egypt comes from a root word meaning 'narrowness', which not only refers to a geographical description of where the country is situated but also connotes a moral, religious and emotional sense as well. The ancient land of Egypt symbolised a place that was narrow-minded; a place where there was only room for us and them; those in power and those who were slaves; those who were of worth and those who were not of equal value. It is said that when Moses and Aaron came to Pharaoh telling him that Yahweh the God of the Israelites demanded that he let them go, Pharaoh consulted his historians, astrologers and counsellors. After searching in their books, they could find no trace of this 'strange god', utterly unknown to them and their sources of knowledge. The Israelites, Christians and Muslims are to 'have no other gods, no strange gods before them'. This God Yahweh has a thing for strangers and anyone who worships Yahweh must imitate God in relating to strangers:

> [God] upholds the cause of the fatherless and the widow, and befriends the stranger, providing him with food and clothing. You too must befriend the stranger, for you were strangers in the land of Egypt.[2]

This is a command, connecting us with all the others. We must act, remembering our own situation when we were in need of freedom, welcome and hope. The basics are to be provided but even more: we are 'to befriend' the stranger, draw them in closer, accept them and treat them as nearer than kin! Whatever our reaction to strangers, its meaning is not found in their presence, but in our hearts. The line before this order to 'befriend the stranger' is startling in its language: 'Cut away, therefore, the thickening about your hearts and stiffen your necks no more' (Deut 10:16). We are interconnected in reality

2. Deut 10:18-19.

and we are not allowed to do anything that gives us a sense of distance, safety or separation from the other. One translation reads: 'Circumcise your hearts, therefore, and be no longer stiff-necked.' To do this, is to obey God and imitate God. The context of this spiritual imperative teaches us about God and about power:

> For the Lord, your God, is the God of gods, the Lord of lords, the great God, mighty and awesome, who has no favourites, accepts no bribes; who executes justice for the orphan and the widow, and befriends the alien, feeding and clothing him. So you too must befriend the alien, for you were once aliens yourselves in the land of Egypt. The Lord, your God, shall you fear, and him shall you serve; hold fast to him and swear by his name. He is your glory, he, your God, who has done for you those great and terrible things which your own eyes have seen. Your ancestors went down to Egypt seventy strong, and now the Lord, your God, has made you as numerous as the stars of the sky.[3]

Earlier in Genesis, the story of Joseph and his brothers tells us that brothers and sisters can become strangers to each other and live as though there are no blood ties. But the other side of that story is found as well: that strangers and aliens can become not only brothers and sisters, but friends. Most of our closest and most intimate relationships – marriage partners and friends – started out as total strangers as Rabbi David J. Wolpe wrote:

> The Joseph story reminds us that biology is no guarantee of closeness and unfamiliarity, no predictor of devotion. It is our task to keep families close and to expand them by including spirits who come to us as strangers and become our kin.[4]

3. Deut 10:16-22.
4. In 'Strangers and Brothers', in *Floating Takes Faith: Ancient Wisdom for a Modern World*, David J. Wolpe, Behrman House, 2004, p. 63.

We must look deep inside ourselves and get beyond our fears in regard to strangers, aliens, refugees, immigrants and just people on the street, in our neighbourhoods, on planes and on the underground. Most of these fears have been created, fanned, manipulated and extended over a long period of time. Since 2001 Americans and many people in the first world have been suffering from mourning sickness and the scourge and plague of shared fear projected on others rather than looking reality in the eye and standing to face it. Rabbi Wolpe writes:

> Many of the ills that afflict us are a product of our creation or our consent. In his journal, Emerson writes, 'Henry [Thoreau] made last night the fine remark that "as long as a man stands in his own way, everything seems to be in his way"'.[5]

As children we lived with fear, especially when we were alone: fear of what lived in the closet or the basement. This is part of growing up. There are marvellous children's books that most adults should re-read, such as *What Was I Scared Of?*[6], in which Doctor Seuss' character is terrified of a pair of green pants. There are other stories too, such as *There's a Monster Under My Bed*. Check the children's section of your local library or bookshop. These stories deal with what adults would call irrational fear, fears that have no basis in reality – they live in our heads, imaginations and psyches. There are valid fears: characteristics and behaviours that may eventually kill us, such as addictions to smoking, which not only adversely affects us but have deadly consequences for others around us; a healthy fear of the consequences of breaking the law stops us drinking and driving, driving while talking on the phone, or driving over the speed limit, remembering that we share the road with others. We are taught to fear fire, deep water, high winds, open electrical sockets, dangerous just by their presence.

5. 'Do We Afflict Ourselves?' ibid., p. 121.
6. Little Dipper Books, Random House for Young Readers, 1997.

In history, every country is afraid of some other country; every people afraid of another people. In the book of Exodus, the new king who comes to power, who does not know Joseph and his history in the country, begins by sowing fear among his subjects:

> Look how numerous and powerful the Israelite people are growing, more so than we ourselves! Come, let us deal shrewdly with them to stop their increase; otherwise, in time of war they too may join our enemies to fight against us, and so leave our country.[7]

The Israelites are, by decree, made internal enemies. They are made to build, toil and work for little or nothing in the supply cities of Pharaoh and they are oppressed. 'The Egyptians, then, dreaded the Israelites and reduced them to cruel slavery, making life bitter for them with hard work in mortar and brick and all kinds of field work – the whole cruel fate of slaves' (Ex 1:13-14). When that doesn't work, the decree to kill all the boy children is enacted. When Israel becomes a nation, it too fears other countries with armies that are larger and more sophisticated than their small one. The prophets alternate between trying to calm the fears of both the leaders and the people of Israel and demanding that they worship only God – for only the true God who is the God of life and truth is real. They are told that their fears of 'what if' or 'they're going to destroy us, invade us, enslave us, take our property and lands' is worshipping strange gods and letting their own fears destroy their covenant with God. Their unfounded fears will lead them into decisions and actions that make their fears come true. The prophets keep asking the people: 'What are you so scared of?'

There is an Arab story from the middle ages, set in Baghdad, that reminds us of how universal fear is and what it can do to us if left unchecked or unquestioned.

Once upon a time a man was on a journey. He set off across

7. Ex 1:9.

the desert, heading towards Baghdad, with food, water and covering for shelter. It was a long, arduous and dangerous journey but he had done it before and he would meet others making the same journey on their business. A couple of days into the desert he saw someone coming towards him, staff in hand. As the heat haze cleared and they drew closer to each other, he was barely able to walk in his terror. It was the Plague that approached him. Plague greeted him warmly and said, 'Oh, you're leaving Basra. That's wise'. The man responded, 'Oh, why, are you going there? What are you going to do there?' He couldn't believe that those words came out of his mouth, with his tongue so dry.

Plague had a sly smile on his face: 'Oh, I'm going to slay 5,000 people.' Suddenly the man felt sick, but the Plague went on its way to the city he had just left. He thought of his friends, business acquaintances and family, and wondered if he should turn around and go to warn them. He prudently decided that would not be a wise move and continued on with his journey to Baghdad. He arrived and set about his work. News of his home trickled in, as the plague slowly spread through the city. As the weeks passed, the numbers rose and people were told to avoid any travel. Word was that they were burning bodies and imprisoning anyone who tried to leave the city. He worried about his family and friends, and prayed they would be alright. With each passing week, the numbers of the dead rose. It was a catastrophe, thousands and tens of thousands – fifty thousand! The man thought to himself that Plague had lied to him. And then, as quickly as it had started, it was over. People began arriving both with horror stories and with stories of being saved. The man decided to return to Basra to see how those he knew were faring.

He gathered his belongings, put his affairs in order and set out, anxious to get home and yet fearful of what he would find there. He was well into the desert and moving quickly when he saw someone approaching. The person looked familiar and he realised with horror that it was the Plague again! Plague walked up to him and leered in recognition. 'Oh, my friend, we meet again – leaving Baghdad?' The man couldn't speak and just nodded his head. 'Wise move on your part.' Before the man realised it, words were spilling out of his mouth. 'You lied to me!' Plague looked pained. 'Me, lie? You are mistaken.' The man blurted out, 'You said you were going to Basra and you were going to take 5,000 people. You lied. The numbers were horrific, more like 50,000 or more. You lied.' Plague looked at him and the man wondered about that look – was it sadness? Plague said, 'I did not lie. I took only the 5,000. All the others died of fright.' And he bowed to the man, and continued on his way to Baghdad. The man stood there, stricken, in the desert.

How do we deal with social and public fears, especially fear that is heightened by laws, administrative guidelines and procedures; and a consistent and calculated intent to blame others for what happens to us, and around us? How do we refuse to succumb to the herd mentality that accepts without question what the media, a government or the leaders of any institution say about others, about groups of people, based on race, ethnicity, language, culture, religion, nationality or physical characteristics and dress? How do we resist the idols of fear that are used to defend economic, political and nationalistic decisions and actions that shut down doors of dialogue, single out peoples as potentially harmful and dangerous, profiling them and lumping them together because of the actions of a few that they have nothing to do with, except that perhaps they share superficial outward characteristics?

Perhaps there are two virtues and practices that we must be introduced to and begin, with others, to live out. The first is that of mourning and grieving for the painful life experiences that do happen, and the other is the attitude and practice of hospitality.

Many of our cultures suffer from a loss of knowing how to mourn. We are expected to get over things quickly, get on with our usual life and routines, repress expressions of our feelings, and just 'get on with it'. But when we do not grieve or cannot mourn, we attack. We blame others, we scapegoat, we want to get even, we want revenge, we want to hide and we want others to pay. We do everything in our power, illogically and irrationally, to make ourselves feel secure because we cannot bear the reality of loss, of truth and vulnerability. What happens is that we become steeped in sadness and depression and a deadly silence pervades our relationships and lives.

We must learn to weep, even howl and to collapse physically, to sob and to let all the feelings and emotions loose, either in private or with others. Our religions must find ways to do this public grieving, in lamentations and songs; in shared silences and in rituals. In Japan and other Asian countries, people place candles in small paper boats with the names of loved ones and release them to float down rivers and streams, taking not only the names, but some of their grief with them as they go. Others fly kites with pieces of paper tied to their tails naming all their fears and things that are preventing them from flying free – then they let them go. We could plant trees in honour of those we love and lose, even if it means groves of trees in our inner cities and downtown areas, all along our streets. (It is not by chance alone that the word 'street' bears within it the word 'tree'!)

In Matthew's account of Jesus' beginnings, Jesus, Joseph and Mary are political and national refugees, immigrants and illegal aliens in Egypt. Fleeing Herod, they return to the original place of bondage, knowing their peoples' history of being strangers, slaves and migrant workers. The short piece that tells the story of Herod's fear of just one child and what one child might do to him and his kingdom is heart-rending. Jesus escapes when Joseph obeys and they run for their lives, across boundaries and borders. But others do not escape. All the families who have children under two years old are attacked and their children slaughtered, families and a village

(Bethlehem) decimated and destroyed. History repeats itself in every corner of the world still. A short phrase from the book of Jeremiah must suffice to try and describe the horror, the weeping and grieving that is expressed. And such weeping has never ended:

> A voice was heard in Raman, sobbing and loud lamentation;
> Rachel weeping for her children, and she would not be consoled, since they were no more.[8]

How did Joseph and Mary grieve? Did they sob terrified and uncontrolled? Did they cling to each other, clutching their child? Did they tell the story of how so many died and he was saved? Did their hearts ache for all those mothers and fathers that cannot be comforted and had to live daily with the reality that 'their children were no more'? We must grieve and weep not only for our own kin and friends, but for all those who are bound to us, loosely, by geography, history, life shared day to day. We must honour their memory by living with their souls and spirits, and sharing their hearts in the choices we make and the lives we live. It is a burden that is precious, light and freeing – to live with the power and presence of those who are lost, especially when they were young or by violence. But we only honour them when we live consciously, instilling their life into the world around us. We never honour another's life when we kill, attack or harm others in blind reaction, in grief that is not expressed.

Once, when I was in Japan visiting at a Zen monastery in Kyoto, there was a question-and-answer period after the practice of bowing, of doing innumerable prostrations, a ritual of standing, slowly bending down to the floor and going prone, then slowly rising again, repeated sometimes up to one hundred times. A novice monk asked the teacher, Roshi Kobun Chino, about the significance of these prostrations. He replied with a story. He told the novice that when his father died he

8. Mt 2:18, cf. Jer 31:15.

was only about eleven years old. He was expected to take over his father's place and to be a support for his mother and the rest of the family. When he was alone in his room he fell on the floor, weeping and sobbing with uncontrollable grief. When he was spent and exhausted he slowly rose and stood looking out the window of his room. He said, 'In that moment, standing after falling and crying like I never had before, I was different. But the whole world was different too. I could go on, absorbing the love I had for my father, even some of my father's spirit into my body and my life. I think of bowing that way each time I do it, now ritually. You go down and when you come back up again, mindfully, slowly gathering all of reality that you can bear within you, you're different. And the world has changed too. We must learn grieving as integral to our life, like breathing and laughing.'

Another crucial aspect of grieving is to tell our stories, to talk – to family and friends, co-workers, even strangers – of what has happened and what it's doing to us now. There is a most remarkable custom among the tribes of north-western Canada and Alaska. It is done only in the month of February and they fervently hope that they will not have to do the rituals for survival each year. When the food runs short the whole village gathers together. The remaining food is collected and, from the beginning of the ritual until the food runs out, the hunters bring in the new game or the women find the new shoots, the villagers all come together for two meals a day, morning and evening. But it is only the children (those under the age of twelve) and the strongest (those who are able to find food for the others) that eat. While they eat, the others are asked to tell their stories. Each speaks of their families and love, dreams and hopes, losses and fears, and each is listened to intently by all the others: those who do not eat and those who do eat. They have learned with ancient wisdom that stories feed souls and spirits, hearts and minds even more than food can feed bodies. Very few of those who do not eat ever die. They say it is because they share common experiences, hopes, fears and the future. They sustain each other.

When I once told this to a group of people in Burma they all looked at each other knowingly and then one of the oldest people in the room stood up and told me that in their traditions in Asia this practice is called 'Holding the Tiger by the Tail'. This is the story they told me.

Once upon a time a young man was travelling. Since the journey was long, he sat down in the heat of the day under a tree, laying his walking staff beside him, and fell asleep. When he woke in the cool of the evening, he reached out with his hand and grasped what he thought was his walking stick. He realised with horror that it was the tail of a tiger. He sprang to his feet but he knew he couldn't let go of the tiger's tail or the tiger would attack him. So he was stuck there.

The tiger growled and roared but the man held on – what else could he do? After a long while, when he thought he would have to give up, he saw a monk walking by on the path and he called out to him to come and help him. The monk came and the man told him, 'Grab my walking stick, kill the tiger, and free me'. But the monk replied, 'I cannot kill. I am a monk'. The man begged and pleaded but the monk kept saying, 'No, it's against my beliefs'. Then the man, in his desperation, had an idea: 'Here, you take the tail of the tiger and I'll kill him.' The monk agreed. They carefully switched places and soon the monk had the tiger by the tail. The man was so relieved he sat down on the ground shaking, massaging his hands and trying to get his breathing back to normal. Then he stood up, got his walking stick and started to leave! The monk panicked, yelling at him, 'Where are you going? You said you'd kill the tiger!' And the man looked at him and said, 'I'm so sorry, it's against my beliefs. I will not kill the tiger either'.

At this point everyone was laughing. The poor monk doesn't come off looking too good in this account. He won't kill, but he doesn't seem to mind that someone else might and doesn't examine his own beliefs until he is suddenly in a different position altogether. One of the old women spoke to me then on behalf of the group, saying: 'What the monk doesn't know is that the man leaves him holding the tiger's tail while he goes off to find people to come and help. You can only hold on alone to the tiger's tail so long. It just depends on your personal strength. In order to let go of the tiger's tail, you need others.' I was waiting for the story's end now. The old man continued.

The man came back within a short time with all the people in the nearest village. They had not dealt with this before but they had talked together on the way and had figured out something they could try. First they got a rope, good and tough, and wrapped it around one of their strongest, who in turn wrapped it around another and another and another. The young man and the monk watched in fascination and in fear. The first man with the rope slowly moved alongside the monk and quietly told him: whatever you do don't let go. The tiger was growling and pulling. Others in the community started throwing small pieces of raw meat at the tiger's feet and he started eating. The man tied one end of his rope around the tiger's tail and held onto the rope, letting the monk go free. The people started feeding the meat to the tiger at farther intervals, pulling the tiger forward while the man let out the rope on the other end. When his segment of rope was gone, the next man began, and the next and the next. Soon the tiger was close to the forest and the people who had strewn pieces of meat on a path into the forest were back near the village. The tiger went into the forest and the people went back home. Eventually the tiger gnawed free of the rope and one of the villagers retrieved it.' Ingenious! When the story was done everyone looked very satisfied and pleased – as though they had themselves come up with the idea – which I guess in reality they did.

In order to deal with certain realities such as tigers, you

have to start thinking and acting like a tiger. Later I was told a Tibetan proverb. It says: 'It is better to live for one day as a tiger, than to live for a thousand years as a sheep.'

In telling our stories to each other, in listening, we learn wisdom not only for the future but for our immediate present. We must, in reality, invite others – all those others, those strangers, those aliens, immigrants, refugees and people we are unfamiliar with and so often afraid of – to tell their stories.

The other virtue that teaches us not only to resist being influenced by the atmosphere of fear that is encouraged in our world is that of hospitality. In the Jewish community this is one of the highest virtues. In practically all religions, the monk or the person who is publically religious is to be treated with hospitality and respect, and honoured as the presence of the Holy in our midst. They, in turn, are to practice hospitality towards all who come to their houses.

The renowned Trappist monk, Thomas Merton, said that he spoke not only for monks, but for every strange 'marginal'. The monk deliberately withdraws to the margins and edge of society with 'a view to deepening fundamental human experience'.[9]

There are many others forced to the edge, pushed into corners and excluded from living with those who say a place only belongs to them. A Carmelite nun, Constance Fitzgerald, OCD writes:

> As Americans we are not educated for impasse, for the experience of human limitation and darkness that will not yield to hard work, studies, statistics, rational analysis, and well-planned programs. We stand helpless, confused, and guilty before the insurmountable problems of our world. We dare not let the full import of the impasse even come to complete consciousness. It is just too painful and too destructive of national self-esteem. We cannot bear to let ourselves be totally

9. *The Monastic Way: Ancient Wisdom for Contemporary Living: A Book of Daily Readings*, ed. Hannah Ward and Jennifer Wild, Canterbury Press, England, 2006.

challenged by the poor, the elderly, the unemployed, refugees, the oppressed; by the unjust, unequal situation of women in a patriarchal, sexist culture; by those tortured and imprisoned and murdered in the name of national security; by the possibility of the destruction of humanity ...

We do not really believe that if we surrender these situations of world impasse to contemplative prayer that new solutions, new visions of peace and equality, will emerge in our world. We dare not believe that a creative re-visioning of our world is possible...Death is involved here – a dying in order to see how to be and to act on behalf of God in the world.[10]

We restore our faith in others and our own balance and humanity with hospitality, shared stories and food. We do it by attending to our own grieving and by honouring those we love and lose by 'living their lives for them' through relating to people they might have reached out to and become friends with. Our communal identity as people (as those sharing a religious belief, ethnic identity, racial heritage or national hope) is fed by imitating our God of life, welcome and freedom. It is nourished by bringing others in from exile, from the edge, and by being people of hospitality. This begins long before we actually eat with another or invite others into our homes and houses of worship. It begins by praying for them, welcoming them into our presence as we go before our God.

We practice contemplating them, as strange as we might find them, so that we can better see our strange God who is flesh and blood among us, hidden under the appearances of many we are unfamiliar with, unaware of, wary of and afraid of. My definition of contemplation is simple: alone and with others, contemplation is a long, loving look at reality, especially reality we find hard to look at. Perhaps in our day

10. 'Impasse and Dark Night', in Tilden H. Edwards (ed.) *Living with Apocalypse: Spiritual Resources for Social Compassion*, Harper and Row, 1984.

and age, it is best practised with others, since we have a tendency to list heavily in the direction of over-identification with individualism. There is a startling and revelatory piece by Eduardo Galeano, an Uruguayan author, historian and storyteller. It is a good story to stay with for a while.

Once upon a time there was a linguist called Carlos Lenkersdorf. He revelled in how people express themselves and how peoples communicate. One day, in the summer of 1972, he was invited to participate in an assembly of Tzetzal Indians in the town of Bachajon. He was delighted at the prospect of hearing a totally different language, a new one for him, an ancient one in reality. It was extremely different from anything he had heard before and he didn't understand even one word of what they were saying. It was just as fascinating for him to sit and listen, and watch them speaking to each other. The discussions grew more intense and heated and the volume rose. 'To him [it] sounded like crazy rain. The word "tik" came through the downpour. Everyone said it, repeated it – *tik, tik, tik* – and it's pitter-patter rose above the torrent of voices. It was an assembly in the key of *tik*.'

Carlos had studied several languages from books and from visiting and living among many groups, primitive tribes and sophisticated peoples. He had studied patterns of communication, worked extensively with translators and had learned some basics that were universal among these speakers, no matter the language employed. In all these languages the word that was most used by everyone, in every sound and level of intensity imaginable was the word 'I'. So as he listened, he logically intuited that the word 'tik' meant 'I' in their language. He listened more closely, watching who was using the word, what their place in the group was and what it sounded like in the mouths of different people. At the end of a long day and night, he finally asked someone who was bi-lingual to confirm his observations. 'The word "tik", as in most other languages, is one word that's used more often than others. It means "I" doesn't it?' The man, who was native Tzetzal, looked horrified. 'No,' he said, 'it doesn't mean that at all. "Tik" [the word that shines at the heart of the sayings and doings of these Mayan communities] means "We".'

When I told this story in Peru, the native peoples nodded – they rarely use the word 'I'. When 'I' is used, it is usually only to ask forgiveness because, as individuals, they have behaved badly in some way and dishonoured their people.

We must, in all our spiritualities, religious practices and education, learn that we are one and that each of us belongs to 'we' and 'us'. This is our root, our foundation and our hope now and in the future.[11]

Practice

Make a list of all the groups of people you consider to be 'strangers, aliens', those we have a tendency to lump into an anonymous blob. Across from them, list all the groups you consider you belong to. Talk to people from one of the groups you 'belong' to. Then make plans to meet someone from the 'other' group so that you can, over time, get to know them as actual people.

Study what the media says about this group of people and at the same time check a concordance in the Bible and other holy books and see what each has to say about this particular group. Think of God or Jesus as a member of that group. How would you react to knowing that this is God present among us today? What do you think your God/our God would have to say about this group now and how they are treated?

Sit quietly and think about who you have wept for – who are they? What do they tell you about yourself and your relation to them? What have you lost besides their presence? How do you live with their spirit in you since they have died? What more would you like to add to your life that reflects their life, their love and their belief?

11. A version of this story originally appeared in *Voices of Time: A Life in Stories*, Eduardo Galeano, trans. Mark Fried, Metropolitan Books, Henry Holt, 2006.

8 FEAR OF THE EARTH, THE WEATHER AND THE UNIVERSE

Le cúnamh Dé agus na dea-uaine.
With the help of God and fine weather.
Dar brí na gréine is na gealaí.
By the power of the sun and the moon.

Lá na seach sion – gaoth mhór, baisteach, sioc agus sneachta, tintreach, toirneach agus lonru gréine.
On the day of seven weathers, there is high wind, rain, frost and snow, thunder, lightning and sunshine.[1]

All of us grow up with proverbs about the weather. My father was in the Navy so one of the first things we learned was: Red sky at morning, sailors warning; red sky at night, sailors delight. Where I live in New Mexico the old say: Don't plant until after the middle of May and invariably spring comes early in February for a week or two, and then just as surely we get a snowstorm in Holy Week, even when it's late. Folks pray for good weather for things as silly as a ballgame or an outing and they pray in novenas for protection from the weather and how earth and sky interact: hurricanes, tornadoes, snow storms, tsunami, wind, lightning strikes, earthquakes and so on. There is even a weather channel that runs twenty-four hours a day so that you can know the weather in any part of the world. It also covers and re-covers the disasters that are connected to

1. Old Irish sayings.

weather and earth's patterns of rotation. We watch the weather nightly, or catch it on our computers so that we think we know what's going to affect us for the next day. Even insurance companies have a whole category of calamities that are dubbed 'acts of God'. They are all connected to what happens with earth, sky, water, wind and weather that affects us and our lifestyles unexpectedly – trees or electrical wires falling down, flooding from torrential rains, ice storms, lack of rain and drought that whips up massive forest fires that invade neighbourhoods and arbitrarily takes some houses, leaving others unscathed.

In the past most peoples were more in touch with day-to-day changes of seasons, as well as being aware of the unusual – storms and eclipses of the sun, moon and tides. Such awareness was necessary for planting, harvesting and indeed for survival itself. Stories abound that are rooted in passing on crucial information from generation to generation. However, in the last fifty years human beings have grown apart from earth and sky and the natural world, relying on technology to alter the seasons, even darkness and light, drastically so that we can live without recourse to what is going on in the world outside. In the past couple of decades many of these realities have been spoken about in terms of global warming and climate change. They have been attributed in large part to the practices of human beings who are both intrigued and frightened of weather that cannot be controlled, in denial about change or seeking to alter the patterns and cope with the consequences that daily impinge on our lives.

It seems that people are becoming more and more afraid of the universe, its vastness and its dwarfing of the human species. That fear is brought close with the numbers of natural disasters that daily assault us in the news or in our own backyard. We, humans, who were created on the sixth day in the stories of Genesis along with all the wild and tame animals and were described as 'very good' in relation to all else in the created universe, are now seen to be out of balance with the rest of creation. Through our neglect and exploitation of natural resources we are even in the process of destroying the earth we depend on. Jesuit priest, palaeontologist and mystic Pierre Teilhard de Chardin wrote: 'The age of nations is past. The task before us now, if we would not perish, is to build the Earth.' These words were written in the middle of the last century, long before we started looking at the earth around us, our landscapes and biospheres, and wondering where we fit into the larger scheme of things.

We are being forced once again to look at where we stand and take heed of where we live and dwell. Martin Buber wrote these words: 'There is something that can only be found in one place. It is a great treasure, which may be called the fulfilment of existence. The place where this treasure can be found is the place on which one stands.'[2]

As rudimentary as it might sound, we have to go back to living consciously on the earth and not in artificial worlds of our own making. What is happening to us as humans is also impacting all other creatures – fish, birds, animals, trees, plants, flowers, the soil, air, water – and thus getting into our food and drink. All seem to be imperilled, in danger of extinction or pollution, and in need of protection. We need radical changes in how we live and how we use the resources we have been given in trust, sharing in God's continued connection to creation that is all good. We seem to have forgotten that throughout the history of revelation God has sought to remind us that we exist in relation to and with all else in the universe. When Moses approaches the burning bush to face God he is first reminded of where he stands: 'Remove the sandals from your feet, for the place on which you stand is holy ground' (Ex 3:5). The ground and all else is holy in the sight of God and we need to keep that in mind as we pursue our lives and our relationships with one another and with the Holy One.

2. *The Way of a Man: According to the Teachings of Hasidism*, Martin Buber, Cloister Press, 1951.

In Genesis 9:8-17 God interacts with Noah and his descendants (and so, with us too) and makes a covenant with all human beings and all our offspring to come and 'with every living creature that is with you – birds, cattle, and every wild beast as well – all that have come out of the ark, every living thing on earth'. The sign of that covenant is the rainbow, the arching bridge between ground and sky in a splash of light and colour. God remembers and we are to remember our bonds as well. The covenant includes the air, waters, earth, resources – everything created – along with us. It seems our God holds us accountable for what transpires on earth and for whether earth thrives or is depleted during our dwelling here. There is a marvellous psalm (148) that is an ongoing litany of all that praises the Holy One, the Creator – we are among the last on the list to join our praises and songs to the symphony. Nothing is excluded from the list – even sea monsters and the weather and natural forces. Obviously all these have languages we do not speak (though in primitive ages, the stories say we all understood one another) but they praise through their essence and their existences – just by being and continuing to be what they were created to be. Psalm 19:2-5 says it aptly:

> The heavens are telling the glory of God;
>   and the firmament proclaims His handiwork.
> Day to day pours forth speech, and night to night
>   declares knowledge.
> There is no speech, nor are there words; their voice
>   is not heard;
> yet their voice goes out through all the earth,
> and their words to the end of the world.

This idea continues throughout the Bible. In the book of Job we read: 'The morning stars chanted in unison, and all divine beings shouted for joy.' My Nana used to tell me that the stars sang and that you could hear 'the crack of dawn' if you were up early enough and were quiet enough. It seems that everything was created for praise, for revelation and for joy! What has happened?

We are creatures torn by awe and wanting to rough it in the wilderness, trek through deserts, scale the highest peaks, kayak in the Artic (now even swim because the water is warming so quickly) and yet we live with an underlying terror that the universe and all that is not human is somehow dangerous and out to get us. This shows up clearly in science-fiction books where practically anything or anyone that comes from 'out there' is not only dubbed alien, but a threat, intent on destroying us, so we apply all the terminology of an enemy to what is totally unknown.

We have forgotten that until very recently we were very low on the food chain in the universe. We are so human – a mix of fear, awe, delight, joy and terror – it has always been so. I found this remarkable poem when I was travelling in Alaska:

> The great sea has set me in motion
> setting me adrift
> moving me like a weed in a river.
> The sky and strong wind
> have moved the spirit inside me
> till I am carried away
> trembling with joy.[3]

There is a Sufi story in the Islamic tradition that states clearly where we find ourselves today in what was once the garden God shared with all of us.

Once upon a time there was a king who went hunting one day. He was separated from his companions, caught nothing and late in the day was thirsty. He came upon a small garden and asked the gardener for a drink. The man responded with hospitality and went immediately to get something to refresh him, not knowing he was the king – he would do the same for

3.   Uvavnuk, a Siberian shaman.

anyone in need. He went to the back of his orchard, picked some pomegranates and squeezed out a cup of juice. He returned almost immediately and gave it to the king to drink. He emptied the cup in seconds and was still thirsty and asked for another cup. Again the gardener went to the orchard to pick more pomegranates.

While the gardener was gone the king started thinking. This man must be rich, and this garden and lands rich. It took only moments for him to return with a cup of pomegranate juice. I didn't know about this place. I should impose a tax on this place and a levy on its produce so that I can profit from it.

While he was thinking about what he would do he realised that the gardener was a lot slower in returning with his second cup. The time went on and he became annoyed. After a good hour the gardener returned with the cup, only half full this time, and the king drank it down as quickly as before. Then he demanded an explanation – why so quickly the first time and so slowly the second time. The man answered saying there were only so many pomegranates ripe at one time in the orchard and there was a time for each thing. 'I had to search for them.'

Then the man, who was really a Sufi master, continued: 'And besides you didn't even appreciate the first cup, gulping it down. You gave no thanks. You just wanted more and you wanted it quickly. When you were first thirsty you were just thirsty but when it took longer to satisfy your thirst your intention shifted and you began to get greedy, thoughtless and unappreciative, thinking only of yourself and what you could do with this place. Your heart was no longer true. I can think of no other explanation for the sudden diminishment of pomegranates, their juice and their reluctance to give themselves for your want.' And he left the king.

Perhaps most of us in the first world find ourselves needing to be told the truth about ourselves and our ways in the world. It is notable that all three of the Synoptic Gospels (Mark,

Matthew and Luke) have accounts of the disciples being terrified when a storm comes up on the sea of Galilee and Jesus, awakened by the disciples, rises to face the wind and waves, calming the elements with a word. Perhaps this short account can give us courage and insight into how to look at our place in the world in relation to the elements and to weather that is out of our control.

> He got into a boat and his disciples followed him. Suddenly a violent storm came up on the sea, so that the boat was being swamped by waves; but he was asleep. They came and woke him, saying, 'Lord, save us! We are perishing.' He said to them, 'Why are you terrified, O you of little faith?' Then he got up, rebuked the winds and the sea, and there was great calm. The men were amazed and said, 'What sort of man is this, whom even the winds and the sea obey?'[4]

The story begins simply and unassumingly enough. Jesus leads and gets into the boat. This is important to remember, that the Creator and the one who sustains all things is with us in the boat, no matter the weather or what happens in the natural world. Jesus is tired and so immediately falls asleep, like a child falls asleep in a rocking cradle or chair, or on a train, lulled by weariness and the movement. A storm immediately comes up. There are many places in the world, inland seas and lakes, as well as the ocean, where storms can seem to come out of nowhere with ferocity, when everything seems to let loose at once. This is a description of weather but it is also a description of what happens in the world with economic collapses, violent conflicts raging all around, and the winds of adversity battering unexpectedly from all sides.

The disciples immediately start to panic and rush to wake Jesus, crying out to him: 'Lord, save us. We are perishing!' They make no effort to secure the boat, rigging, sails or other

4. Mt 8:23-27.

equipment in order to ride out the storm. Instead they wake Jesus, who seems oblivious to the mayhem around them. They jump to the conclusion that they are going to die, right there and then. They pray, but it's the prayer of panic, terror and desperation born of blind inability to control the situation. (In our world there is cause for a lot of that kind of basic praying.) Jesus rebukes them and chastises them about their panic, their lack of faith or awareness of what is happening and their jumping to the worst possible conclusion. He asks them bluntly: 'Why are you afraid?' It is a good question that we all need to start with. Why are we afraid of the weather, of the forces of the universe or powers that are beyond our control? The underlying roots of our fear have to be faced before we can do anything except aggravate the situation rather than endure it or help others ride it out. There are going to be endless situations we are going to have to face and the response of fear is not necessarily the one we should initially succumb to. Jesus continues and calls them in a group: 'O you of little faith!'

What groups do we belong to – and do they contribute to our fears and our lack of faith? Do we insist on hanging around with and continuing our behaviours, encouraged by others, when to do so is only to avoid the reality? Sometimes the company we keep is far worse than the climate around us! In this situation faith is a way of being, a way of attending to the world and a state of mind that remembers first that we are not at the mercy of the world – the Creator of the world is with us and while there is danger and sometimes good reason to fear, we are not to be consumed by it as a first response.

Jesus gets up, stands upright in the boat, holding his balance, and then rebukes the wind and the sea. His words evoke a great calm. It seems that the weather responds and it leaves us wondering if the disciples respond as well, settling down and looking at the world differently through the eyes of Jesus. Their attention shifts from the storm to the person standing with them in the boat and they begin to ask another question: 'What sort of man is this, whom even the winds and the sea obey?' The question is phrased carefully – what sort of man is this that even forces of nature obey him? We need to ask the same questions of ourselves. What sort of human beings, men and women, are we that we stand in the world, balanced, and evoke obedience and calm from the elements and forces around us? Jesus is adept at facing reality, standing with courage, with heart and attention before the world all ways, at all times and in all weathers and circumstances. Are we? What gives us balance? What foundational reality do we stand on always no matter the outward climates and situations? What do we put our 'little' faith in – science, technology, superstitions, apathy and refusal to look at reality all around us, denial, seeing every incident and experience as an opportunity for profit, solidification of our own place? What kind of men and women are we? Are we holy – meaning whole, of one piece, balanced, in right relationship to everyone and everything, including the world we live in?

This story isn't just about being caught in a weather pattern but about being in the world. In a collection of sayings by contemporary monks I found this interesting reflection for 14 October by Frances Teresa OSC:

> Without doubt, holiness is our greatest ecological contribution. Without it, we shall never balance the needs and rights of our diversified world. Holiness is restoration of order in its most searching and creative form, an unfailing source of respect for others. The reason why Francis [of Assisi] is such an appropriate patron for ecological movements is not so much because he preached to the birds and rescued worms from the dangers of the road, but because he approached all that is made with a respect bordering on reverence.[5]

5. *The Monastic Way: Ancient Wisdom for Contemporary Living: A Book of Daily Readings*, ed. Hannah Ward and Jennifer Wild, Canterbury Press, 2007

Jesus is holy, of course, in right relationship to everything. To our peril now in the human community, this sort of holiness has been the primary focus of very few human beings since Jesus. Perhaps Jesus was admonishing his disciples about their own relation to the universe, their own lack of awareness of their being in the world, and so their fear could be triggered by any number of things – from a storm on the lake to the murmurings of people disturbed by his presence in the world.

They were in need of holy fear – being afraid of what can destroy and being in awe of what is more powerful and good than what is normally accepted in society.

It seems that this fact seeps through all of reality. There is holy fear that brings forth life and there is destructive fear that short-circuits us from everything around us, even in the natural world of trees and animals. Read this piece in amazement at what is balance and how to bring calm to the world:

Trees thrive off fear

Aspen are particularly tasty to elk and have long suffered from over-browsing in Yellowstone National Park. But now aspen in some areas are making a comeback – thanks to wolves. Though eradicated from Yellowstone in the 1920s, wolves were reintroduced in 1995 and have been multiplying ever since. The result? Elk avoid riversides, where they're particularly exposed to the predator, and there's a whole new crop of young aspen in such areas, according to Oregon State University researchers, who credit the arboreal rebound to the 'ecology of fear'.[6]

It appears that all creation is intended to follow some basic principles of respect and balance that makes the whole world and all its inhabitants holy. Disregarding this ecology of justice throws everything out of kilter. Reintroducing behaviours and

6. *Smithsonian*, October 2007, p. 18.

a good dose of faith, along with appreciating everything on the earth, brings radical changes, even things we didn't realise were all bound together. Since Jesus, perhaps the person most credited with understanding this, in faith, is Francis of Assisi, the patron of ecology and of peace-makers. This quote reveals why Francis' life and faith is so needed as foundational today:

> He never wanted to terminate the life of anything and forbade the brothers to cut down the whole tree when they cut wood for the fire, because the tree too must be allowed the hope of sprouting again. This was not sentimentality but a deep and respectful awareness that nothing existed just for him, as if he were the owner in some way. Rather, he saw the dying and the rising of Christ as the basic story, the foundation event of our planet, and possibly of the universe, and that everything which exists does so within these parameters. The trees, too, must be left with hope of their resurrection. Christ's story is our story and that of our planet, and by our lives, we re-tell it over and over again. We have no right to bring this story to closure in any of its myriad versions.[7]

Both Matthew and Luke tell even more powerful stories of Jesus coming at night to the disciples in the boat, by walking on the water! And all the stories are laced with fear and terror. In Matthew, Jesus invites Peter out onto the water to walk towards him, though he begins quickly to sink! This last piece (Mt 14:22-34) has been described as a drama in four acts and it is meant to be looked at as a symbolic structure of stages of our lives:

> Then he made the disciples get into the boat and precede him to the other side, while he dismissed the crowds. After doing so, he went up on the mountain by himself to pray. When it was evening he was there alone.

---

7. *Living the Incarnation: Praying with Francis and Clare of Assisi*, Frances Teresa, OSC, Darton, Longman & Todd, 1993, p. 90.

Meanwhile the boat, already a few miles offshore, was being tossed about by the waves, for the wind was against it. During the fourth watch of the night, he came towards them, walking on the sea. When the disciples saw him walking on the sea they were terrified. 'It is a ghost,' they said, and they cried out in fear.[8]

This time Jesus is up on a mountain praying and the disciples are in the boat on the sea, separated by place, water and intent. They are going on ahead of him and he is staying still. Now the disciples spend the night struggling in the middle of the sea: they can't go back and they can't seem to go forward either because they are in the face of the wind. They are far from land but this wind, this ruah, Yahweh is pushing against them is the same wind that swept across the face of the deep waters at creation. This is life. Sometimes we feel like we are going nowhere, hung between what was and what is no longer, but we can't even see the further shore.

And at the fourth watch – early in the morning, around that hour of the tiger time – Jesus comes to them walking on the water! They think it is a ghost and are terrified. They have spent the night in fear and dread, just trying to keep from capsising and drowning and are worn ragged. Jesus treads the waters of the sea. (This has echoes of Jesus trampling down death in the ancient accounts of the resurrection. Or it is the echo of treading the wine press of suffering and of making wine from grapes for celebration and joy. It is on water, but treading the paths up mountains and along the seashore and in deserts, each in their own way, are sometimes hard paths to tread.) He does not let them drown in their fear for even a moment.

He speaks with power, authority and strength, immediately diverting them from fear to shock and awe:

At once Jesus spoke to them, 'Take courage, it is I; do not be afraid'. Peter said to him in reply, 'Lord, if it is

8. Mt 14:22-27.

133

you, command me to come to you on the water'. He said, 'Come'. Peter got out of the boat and began to walk on the water toward Jesus. But when he saw how [strong] the wind was he became frightened; and beginning to sink, he cried out, 'Lord save me!' Immediately Jesus stretched out his hand and caught him, and said to him, 'O you of little faith, why did you doubt?' After they got back into the boat, the wind died down.[9]

What Jesus says is astounding: 'it is I' or, in Greek, '*ego eimi*' meaning 'I AM', the same words that Yahweh uses on the mountain when speaking to Moses and commanding him to go and set the people free from Egypt. I AM is in the world, everywhere. This is the presence of God in human flesh everywhere in the world, in the waters, air, everywhere. This is I AM who is with us until the end of the ages (Mt 28:20), the last words of Jesus in Matthew's gospel that are stirring words of power given over to those who believe in him. Jesus is shouting at them that he is with them even when they do not perceive him or sense his presence and they are terrified. He is not a ghost or the figment of someone's imagination. He exists and is as real as the storm, the waters and the relative safety of the boat they are in. And because of his presence they are to 'take courage', to 'take heart' and not be ruled by their fear ever, anywhere. Because of the mystery of the Incarnation – of God becoming flesh and blood among us, dwelling among us always, God has shared his heart with us in Jesus. We are to lay hold of that heart and live with the courage of God – to face our fears knowing we have the power and the strength of God – or of the tiger within us!

When Peter makes his move – 'let's see if I can do what Jesus does' – he is invited to get out of the boat, beyond his safety net and come towards Jesus. He does, perhaps caught up in the moment, exhilarated and without thinking about what it is he's trying to do. And he walks on water! What

9. Mt 14:27-32.

things are we capable of that appear to break the laws of the universe when it is for moving towards goodness and God?

We need to try to reseed the world, clean the oceans and the air, protect what is endangered, stop extinction, care for human beings so that all live justly and in peace that abides, letting the land rest from war and desecration, so that all the peoples of the world know the beauty and the goodness of what was given to us as a garden. We need to heed the warnings and meanings of weather and climate shifts, and take to heart what the world needs from us so that we are not just enduring the weather and living in fear from the earth, squandering its resources, but living in attentive awareness that we are intimately linked together.

Peter began in doubt with his question, half-heartedly saying 'If you are …', and as soon as he realises the strength of what he is relating to in the waters and wind and currents he slips back into his place of fear – and starts to sink into the water. He takes his eyes off Jesus. He is distracted. He loses his horizon and so, his foot-hold. He forgets who moves the universe, who set all the elements and forces of the earth in motion and sustains everything, including him. And he is back to crying out again as they did earlier while Jesus was in the boat with them: 'Save me!' He is reduced to his lowest grade of fear again, so quickly. The text simply says that Jesus immediately stretched out his hand and caught him – and repeats his words of truth-telling: 'O you of little faith, why did you doubt?' Peter forgets. We all forget so easily that the saving hand of God in Jesus is always there. It does not necessarily keep us from harm or deliver us from suffering and death, but it is a saving hand, because it is always there. As Isaiah the prophet wrote: 'See I have inscribed you on the palms of my hands' (Is 49:16). We are always that close to God, but we have to see – pay attention, heed the presence and not get distracted. Whatever we are doing has to be pointed in the direction of saving others, saving grace and saving earth.

Jesus and Peter get back into the boat – Peter awkwardly (chagrined?) Jesus, gracefully (a smile on his face?). When they are all in the boat again, the storm dies down and the wind lets go its fierce resistance against them. One gets the sense that they are all subdued, thoughtful and taken aback. They have been wrenched out of their usual lives and given a glimpse of a reality that serves the commands of God, resulting in the incredible possibility of a people and a world saved. We are told that those in the boat 'did him homage', acknowledging the right order of the universe, saying the words of belief in the community of Matthew, 'Truly, you are the Son of God' (Mt 14:33).

The story is multi-layered and full of meaning. The boat is often referred to as the church and Peter as leader, though in this accounting and in most others he doesn't come off well as a leader or as anyone to imitate. But perhaps the boat is all of us in the world and we are, so to speak, all in the same boat – this planet earth, this universe we float in along with other planets. This scenario of one getting out of the boat to do something based on 'what if', doubt and individual hubris or greed for power and attention shows the immature motives we are capable of. It might also be a glimpse of what is possible in the universe if our motives are true and we walk in tandem with God. With Peter and Jesus back in the boat – all of us together – there is calm and things can get back to normal, or at least back to what is easier for human beings.

Storms are as necessary as calm, rain as critical as sun, warmth and cold understood in relation to each other. Everything in the universe is necessary and is trying always to right itself, undo the harm and excess of what is happening – like trees seeking to absorb carbon dioxide so that we can breathe easily again. We are meant to face all of this together. God is not going to interfere and stop the climate change or the freak storms or the earthquakes. It is up to us to try to even out and mitigate destruction and stop whatever we are doing that is twisting the patterns of the universe and over-loading what the forces of nature – earth, air, water and all that is created – can take. What we are being told is: take heart, take courage – I AM with you always, here and now, through it all.

This is faith that is not only momentary, but it is lived daily, as endurance, as surely as belief that is attested to. It is being tested, living gracefully in spite of what happens and at the same time saving the earth and each other by doing what we are exhorted to do: take heart, take courage. Sometimes that means hanging on for dear life or hanging on for a dearer life. Always it means to be converted and to transform and undo the harm we have done, trusting that what God has made is good. It means believing in God's presence in Jesus, capable of doing 'even greater things than I' – to redeem and save what is unravelling. Grace persists and endures and is stronger than any fear. Awe is the beginning of seeing what can be done to redeem any situation. Through it all, the Spirit, the driving wind of God, is always present to evoke in us wildly imaginative responses to what we need to do and to what is happening around us. Do not be afraid! Take heart! It is I!

Practice
Watch the weather report on TV, online or in the newspaper for a week and watch your own reactions to what is forecast. Check out what the weather actually is in relation to what was predicted. Also watch for what are described as 'acts of God' – usually weather that is dangerous, life-threatening, out of control. Look around and see what other 'acts of God' there are in connection with weather, the skies, waters, the ground, the stars and discoveries on earth and in the heavens. What does your fear of such things tell you about yourself? Try being aware of the weather and appreciative of it, no matter what it does; see how it is bound up with everything else in the universe. Try to see what it says about the world rather than see it as a problem or something to be changed to fit your agendas and schedule.

9 FEAR OF GOD AND FEAR OF MYSTERY

In the tiger's mouth there are many exquisite jewels.[1]

There is a saying in Judaism that is a bit baffling: 'The fear of the Lord is the beginning of wisdom.' In this sense, fear of God is a gift. It is goodness. It is an invitation beyond where one is standing. It is something to be reached for, grasped hold of and attended to. Yet when we speak of fear we are usually talking about servile fear that reduces us to grovelling, to being paralysed or imprisoned within our minds and hearts. Perhaps this fear of God is all these realities and more. We can fear all that is unknown and the ultimate Unknown is God. We can fear a God that we have been taught exists and lies in wait for us, and is vindictive, judgemental, angry, acting like a petulant parent when annoyed rather than a God of life ever-more abundant for all, a God of justice, truth and peace.

In Christianity when one is confirmed there are seven gifts of the Spirit that are given for public life and witness to one's belief in the world. The last on the list is fear of the Lord. This fear is awe, wonder, a sense of mystery and the unknown as a lure into a farther horizon and another way of perceiving reality. This is the way Albert Einstein described it:

> The most beautiful experience you can have is a sense of the mysterious. It is the fundamental emotion that stands

1. Wisdom saying.

at the cradle of true art and true science. Whoever does not know it and can no longer wonder, no longer marvel, is as good as dead, and his eyes are dimmed.

But this is only the first layer of meaning that directs our gaze outward. There are other more intense, deeper levels that lead both farther afield and within. It is not only an attitude of wonder towards all that is created, but an attitude that essentially reaches towards what created or set in motion everything, or what we call God. This God can be an illusive concept, a catch-all for what we cannot understand or know, or a power that stirs and directs, even participates in all the mysteries of the universe's functioning and existence. It is often the universe itself that initiates the wonder and the questioning of what God might be, as William Jennings Bryan (1860–1925) wrote:

> I have observed the power of the watermelon seed. It has the power of drawing from the ground and through itself 200,000 times its weight. When you can tell me how it takes this material and out of it colours an outside surface beyond the imitation of art, and then forms inside of it a white rind and within that again a red heart, thickly inlaid with black seeds, each one of which in turn is capable of drawing through itself 200,000 times its weight – when you can explain to me the mystery of a watermelon, you can ask me to explain the mystery of God.[2]

Any phenomenon in the universe can trigger this sense of awe that seeks a connection to the maker and the keeper of all things, and to more questions about our relationship and connection to this mystery that we call God. It is said that the root meaning of the word 'god' in any language is simply what sounds like 'huh? uh?' It is at its root the sense of something or

---

2. *Wisdom of the Ages: 60 Days to Enlightenment*, Wayne W. Dyer, Quill, Harper Collins, 1998.

someone questioning us. This sense of Someone ultimately The Unknown or the Indescribable is linked intimately to our sense of impermanence or mortality – that someday we either die and disappear, or die and are drawn into connection with something More. This More is more than each of us and more than all of us, more than history, science, art, more than everything – and this More is somehow bound to the ultimate Truth of all life and existence, or meaning for us who are not, except in relation to this Truth, this Life, this Reality that encompasses all else. This is one way of saying it: you are and so I am. The mystery demands that we look at what might be our relationship to this entity we generally call by the word 'god'.

What about those who claim there is no god, sometimes calling themselves atheists or non-believers for any number of reasons? Even if one does not believe in a Creator or Mover God, as a scientific principle, let alone as a personal God, or if one does not belong to one of the major religions, every one of us does have a 'god'. A god is what we worship, attend to, are devoted to, pay heed to and sacrifice to, put our lives in primary connection with. For believers, this god is often called an 'idol', a false god that stands in opposition to or in conflict with the God named by religions and adherents to a belief system. It can be almost anything: money, power, status, reputation, identity, knowledge/information, science, art, love, sex, another person, our own person, possessions, land, wealth, a group, a corporation, a nation – we are ingenious at taking something and making it our god. We settle for something tangible, graspable because we are reluctant or afraid to reach beyond what is visible and malleable or useful to us. We have deeply rooted fears that are bound to all our small gods. Each reveals a fear to us. Buddhist writer Jack Kornfield says, 'As we willingly enter each place of fear, each place of deficiency and insecurity in ourselves, we will discover that its walls are made of untruths, of old images of ourselves, of ancient fears, of false ideas of what is pure and what is not'. He speaks on a psychological and meditative practice level but his words are accurate for all human beings, whether they claim to believe in God or not.

What if the fear of the Lord is the beginning of wisdom? Another Buddhist, Matthieu Ricard, says, 'Wisdom and compassion should become the dominating influences that guide our thoughts, our words and our actions'.[3]

We are all afraid of this Unknown, this Unnameable, this Indescribable, this God; but is it fear that liberates, frees and demands that we dwell in the Truth or is it fear that subjects us to loneliness, dread and a sense that we are doomed? What follows is a rather strange, disquieting story from the Islamic tradition that questions us about what we seek, what we fear and what might be true fear of the Lord.

Once upon a time there was an Iman by the name of Isa, ibn Maryam. One day as he was travelling he came upon a group of people sitting on a wall in a line. They looked utterly miserable and terrified, each alone in their terror, yet all had the same awful look. He stopped and asked them, 'What is your affliction?' They all answered, 'We are afraid of hell'. He continued on his journey and later saw another group of people all huddled together in small clusters, in strange positions on the ground. They too looked disconsolate and in pain. He asked them how they had gotten into such a state of body and soul. Each group answered him, 'We are just waiting and living for heaven'. He went again on his way. Soon he came upon another group of people. They looked like they had endured much, survived and had lived, but their faces absolutely shone with joy. He came close to each of them, looking into their eyes and faces, and asked each one, 'How did you get this way?' Each answered the same words, but with infinitely diverse expressions on their faces and in their bodies: 'The Spirit of Truth has made us like this! We have caught a glimpse of Reality, of The Truth, and we seek above

3. *Offerings: Buddhist Wisdom for Every Day, Spiritual Wisdom to Change Your Life*, Danielle and Olivier Follmi, photographers of the Dalai Lama, Stewart, Tabori and Chang, 2003.

all else to serve Truth alone. We endeavour to harm no one, to ease suffering and to live with freedom shared with all.' Isa marvelled at them all. These people knew how to live! These people had been touched by a finger of The Truth! These people already lived in the presence of God whether they realised it or not. These people were the gate.

The only time I told this story there were many reactions and many of them were negative, reactive and rejecting everything about the story. It caused a great deal of discussion, dissension and questions about what exactly I was trying to say. I wasn't really trying to say anything in particular. The story had done something to me, stirring a range of reactions, and I sought to see what it did to others. Afterwards a stranger came up to me and said that story is dangerous and that the last line should be: 'These people have passed through the gate of the tiger!' I had talked about tigers and the book I was writing on fear and how we respond in such myriad ways, ways that can be both destructive and imaginative. What if Truth is the gate of the tiger? What if fear of the Lord is the beginning of wisdom and the gate of the tiger? What if Truth, acknowledgement of Mystery that is beyond our comprehension and yet encompasses us, is the beginning of real life, in depth, in expansiveness and in ways of relating to others, being human, that can only be described as like God?

Fear of the Lord states that there is no other fear that is stronger than the fear of not responding humanly and living in obedience to the Lord – or the fear of disappointing God. Fear of the Lord states that the only power that we submit or surrender to is the power of God. For believers in God: The Trinity of the Father who is Life-Giver, the Son, the Word made Flesh dwelling among us and the Spirit, the Wind and Fire of ever-abundant life, imagination and expression. This means that we state with every moment of our lives that we live under no sign of power but this sign of the cross, this sign of the Trinity. We fear no nation, no other, no situation, no loss, no suffering, no loneliness or isolation, no torture, no imprisonment, no humiliation, no lack, nothing, not even death, more than we fear to dishonour God or to betray our obedience to what is good, just, life-giving and true for all. Every moment and every place, every person and every situation is that gate of the tiger, that gate into the Truth.

There is an account in the gospels that appears almost immediately after Jesus tries to tell his disciples that he is going to be rejected and die that is called the Transfiguration. It is an account of mystery, of revelation, of insight and vision. It disturbs us, engenders fear in us and questions us. It describes what a moment of 'fear of the Lord' might be like and its effects on us, immediately, and in the long term. This is Matthew's account:

> After six days Jesus took Peter, James and John his brother, and led them up a high mountain by themselves. And he was transfigured before them, his face shone like the sun and his clothes became white as light. And behold, Moses and Elijah appeared to them, conversing with him. Then Peter said to Jesus in reply, 'Lord, it is good that we are here. If you wish, I will make three tents here, one for you, one for Moses, and one for Elijah'. While he was still speaking, behold a bright cloud cast a shadow over them, then from the cloud came a voice that said, 'This is my beloved Son, with whom I am well pleased, listen to him'. When the disciples heard this, they fell prostrate and were very much afraid. But Jesus came and touched them, saying, 'Rise, and do not be afraid'. And when the disciples raised their eyes, they saw no one else but Jesus alone.[4]

Every phrase is inscribed so that it reveals a piece of knowledge that is crucial. It is an account of mystery, a statement of faith and an attempt to speak about something

4. Mt 17:1-8.

that is almost unbelievable unless you have the gift of faith or the intent to try to be open and glean from the words something of value that just might be the Truth. It begins with the phrase 'after six days'. The whole story is predicated on what has gone before and how it impacted on Jesus and especially these three chosen to go up the mountain. What immediately precedes this experience on the mountain is Jesus' first confrontation with the disciples, especially Peter, who is singled out when Jesus tries to make them face the reality of what is going to happen to him. He is on his way to Jerusalem, the city of peace, also the city of the destruction and death of the prophets. He is brutal in his detailed description of what awaits him if he continues teaching that God is present in the world in his own person and that this God who has come into history is a God of hope and forgiveness who touches with the two hands of justice and mercy. The disciples can't and won't hear what he is saying to them. They are terrified of rejection; terrified of the physical pain of torture, crucifixion and a humiliating death that is so horrible that they believe that a person who dies like that is abandoned even by God. So the story is told and they are brought to the mountain for light, truth and courage – antidotes to their fears.

The story is all about Jesus, the presence and the physical touch and body of God in Incarnation, death and resurrection, and still dwelling among us. It is Jesus who is transformed, transfigured. He becomes all light, power and terrifying in his own right. His face, his clothes, his figure are altered radically. The word transfiguration comes from the Latin 'trans', meaning 'across', 'a bridge to', 'a passage through' – it can even mean 'a gate'. The word 'figure' means 'the human body or person'. The power, light and presence of God comes through the body and person of Jesus and Jesus himself becomes the bridge, the passageway and the gate into God for those moments.

Two others appear with Jesus, Moses and Elijah. In the Jewish community these are the two greatest prophets, figures of their ancient history and hope: the liberator and lawgiver of the people seeking to turn them back to true worship and life as the people of God. They are conversing with Jesus, a dialogue of questioning, answering and seeking to know. We are not told here what it is they are talking about but in other accounts it is about his time in Jerusalem, the cross and his death, which lead into life, resurrection and light. Oddly it says that 'in reply' to this vision, Peter says something rather pedantic and ordinary. That it's good to be here and that he'll set up three tents so that Moses, Elijah and Jesus can stay! Whatever an experience of mystery is, it is good, and our initial reaction is to hang onto it and keep it with us, even if we say or do rather inane things in response.

Peter is interrupted by the movement of a bright cloud that casts a shadow over all of them. It is all of light: light that blinds, silences; stills and terrifies. It is light with presence because it casts a shadow over them – the same words of overshadowing throughout the Bible that announce birth, life and God entering into human beings' lives. This is an echo of God who travelled with the Israelites as fire at night and a cloud by day. Out of the cloud comes a voice that echoes the words of Jesus' baptism as he rose up out of the water. The words are familiar: 'My beloved son, I am delighted and pleased. Listen to him.' They are foundational and state a fact, declare a relation and command obedience. With the cloud, the voice and the body of Jesus, the Trinity is together mysteriously revealing power and knowledge that is the only Truth, the only reality the disciples need to know and heed. They have been listening to the fears of the crowds, fearing the Romans. They have been listening to their own fears and feeding them by talking with each other, but not to Jesus. They have been listening to the fears of those in occupied territory who have made deals to survive and accommodate religion, economics and even a level of politics to survive under a brutal regime. They are consumed by their fears of what might happen, of the unknown and of those with the power they lack. But now it is time to know the power of the fear of the Lord that draws them into wisdom.

Their reaction is one of worship, prostrating themselves on the ground, with no words, no sense even and they are afraid, terrified and know this other kind of fear before Mystery, before the Holy Ones. They have been brought to the gate, to the passageway and to the light, and they see the glory of God shining on the face of Jesus. Then something surprisingly human happens: Jesus comes to them and touches them, his hand on their shoulders, their heads, their outstretched arms, backs and he says: 'Rise, and do not be afraid.' Were the words spoken quietly, reassuringly, intimately? Or were they spoken with strength, authority and power, commanding them, instilling them with his own grace and courage? The first word, 'Rise!' is imperative and points to the resurrection, to the life that begins in baptism and permeates our entire lives with courage, truth and power. It does not stop our very natural and understandable fears, but allays them, undoes their hold on us so that we can rise, walk and become children, servants and beloved of the God of light, mystery and truth. In the closing piece of the story, they raised their eyes, still on the ground, and they see no one else, only Jesus alone. These words have layers of meaning: if we only learn to see Jesus; if we only see Jesus alone; if we only see with Jesus, hear him, listen to him (meaning to obey him) and if we only see through Jesus' eyes, words, face, body and presence to the Truth and the Mystery of what is – then we can rise and stand with courage, knowing what to fear and what is empty and, in the end, subject to Wisdom.

Sometimes when I teach, I remind people that their eyes are connected to their ears. They laugh, but I suggest to them that if they wear glasses or contact lens to notice what happens when they remove them: they find it harder to hear! The same works when we close our eyes and seal off what is happening around us: our hearing dulls and we are removed from what is around us. We escape from reality that impinges upon us. Hearing the voice, the words of God, in one's religious tradition, especially with others, and in ritual settings can sometimes elicit an experience of mystery. This experience of hearing with others is often a place where the edge of mystery is found. Researchers are becoming more and more convinced that what we often refer to as 'mystical experiences or moments' are much more common than we might have once assumed. Finding one's self, and others in our company, at the gate of the tiger, the edge of mystery, is often what happens when we are confronted with fear but enter and pass through it.

What happens after you walk through this gate of the tiger, the passageway of mystery? When I was working on this book and delving into fear of the other, fear of strangers, I found a remarkable statistic: we are told in the book of Leviticus (19:18) only once to love our neighbour, but we are exhorted to love the stranger more than thirty times in early books of the Torah. Somehow opening our door and our eyes and heart to the stranger is opening to mystery, to the Other, to the unknown that always reeks of God. A rabbi once said that God is manifest in every stranger and since we are no longer strangers to God, we cannot be strangers to each other! In fact, he went on to say that loving the stranger and loving God are the same thing, just two ways of honouring the Holy among us. What this means is that hospitality to others (as in the story of Abraham in Genesis 18 when the three strangers come to his tent) is a defining and central piece of our religion, our spirituality and our primary introduction to mystery. It is laced with fear, risk, openness and courage. We must encourage hospitality in one another so that we can walk through the gate of the tiger together often.

Another marvellous thing I discovered was wisdom from Rabbi David J. Wolpe, which he calls 'Normal Mysticism'. Once one has passed through the gate, perhaps even only once, and seeks to live looking for the gates of the tiger, the gates of wisdom, one can become what he calls a normal mystic. This is his short, amazing and fearfully true description of what that could be:

> The scholar Max Kadushin wrote a dense, rich work called *The Rabbinic Mind*. In it he coins a wonderful name for the religious outlook of our sages: he called them 'normal mystics'. A normal mystic does not have hallucinatory visions of celestial glories. A normal mystic does not spend days and nights in ascetic pursuits, conjuring up some other, arcane realm of existence. A normal mystic is not a cave dweller practising secret rituals. He is normal.
>
> Still the tag 'mystic' remains. For a normal mystic is one who better sees, or feels, the shaping and guiding hand of Divinity in all things. No event, whether personal, political or natural, is outside the realm of divine providential concern. The normal mystic is, in the phrase often used to describe the philosopher Spinoza, God intoxicated – drunk with the Divine. An awareness of God seeps into all the activities of human life until this unseen Presence is taken as the true foundation of being, more real than what we glibly dub reality.
>
> To see God in the everyday is the legacy of the Rabbis. Normal mysticism does not escape this world; it elevates it.[5]

I would take it a step or two further. This condition called normal mysticism is the usual way of living without fear, or at least subduing our fears or subsuming them in the fear of the Lord so that we live trusting in God's grace, facing our fears as gates of the tiger and gates into wisdom.

5. *Floating Takes Faith: Ancient Wisdom for a Modern World*, David J. Wolpe, Behrman House, 2004, p. 39.

This wisdom of the Holy can be found lurking everywhere – there is no place where it does not dwell, waiting to be uncovered, found and taken away. We must honour those who keep trying to share it, especially those who find it underneath the fears and terrors and horrors of our world. Here is a piece of what it looks and sounds like – I found it on the back cover of a magazine in Canada called *Briarpatch*:

> I write in the night, but I see not only the tyranny. If that were so, I would probably not have the courage to continue. I see people sleeping, stirring, getting up to drink water, whispering their projects or their fears, making love, praying, cooking something whilst the rest of the family is asleep, in Baghdad and Chicago … I see pastry cooks working in Tehran and the shepherds, thought of as bandits, sleeping beside their sheep in Sardinia. I see a man in the Friedrichshain quarter of Berlin sitting in his pyjamas with a bottle of beer reading Heidegger, and he has the hands of a proletarian. I see a small boat of illegal immigrants off the Spanish coast near Alicante. I see a mother in Mali – her name is Aya, which means born on Friday – swaying her baby to sleep. I see the ruins of Kabul and a man going home, and I know that, despite the pain, the ingenuity of the survivors is undiminished, an ingenuity which scavenges and collects energy, and in the ceaseless cunning of this ingenuity, there is a spiritual, something like the Holy Ghost. I am convinced of this in the night, although I don't know why.[6]

Perhaps our fear of God, or our fear that God looks more like human beings who aren't really very human, or if our image of God is easily manipulated to our own ends – perhaps all this is really the fear that there isn't a God and that we are not created with meaning to be children of light and freedom

6. 'Written in the Night: The Pain of Living in the Present World', John Berger, *Le Monde Diplomatique*, 15 February 2003.

dwelling in truth. When I listen to people they can say, 'What if there isn't a God?' These words do not say that someone is an atheist but rather that they fear that their belief is without substance. This reality is not so much a lack of faith as it is a fear that faith itself is created to keep the unknown at bay.

We all have our fears. In this regard we are about as common and united as humans can be. Often what we fear reveals far more about us than it does about reality. It is truly a gift of the Spirit to fear only the Lord, only the Lord of life and truth, justice, peace and mercy, and to let no other fear rob us of this life that dwells in mystery.

There is another story called 'The Tiger and the Persimmon' (an orange fruit of the persimmon tree), which can impart wisdom, the best kind, that leaves us questioning and wondering, seeking a deeper way into mystery.

Once upon a time there was a tiger that loved to prowl along the edges of the villages and sometimes slip into one, coming up close, right to the windows or doors of a house, to watch human beings as they went about their lives. One very dark night she slipped into a village, unseen, and stopped below a window when she heard a child crying. She was curious. The mother rebuked the child and said, 'Stop your crying right now. A tiger is here and listening to you'. But the child didn't pay any attention. That's what his mother always said, trying to frighten him into behaving or stopping whatever he was doing.

But the tiger thought, 'Hmm ... the child is not afraid of me. I wonder what this child is like'. Then the mother continued, trying to make the child stop his crying: 'Here, take this persimmon and stop your crying right now.' The child stopped crying immediately and took the persimmon. Now this frightened the tiger! A persimmon! The child is afraid of a persimmon and obeys and takes it – what kind of creature is this persimmon. With that the tiger decided to leave the child alone and certainly to avoid this thing called a 'persimmon'!

There is more to this tiger and persimmon story, but we will save it for the next chapter. What do we fear? Does it control us? Do we even know what it looks like? It is good to be afraid of some things – fear can save our lives and it can form our consciences or give us the courage to be more truthfully human in imitation and obedience to our God. Perhaps it is wisdom to know a holy fear that demands that we live with courage and that we all live together truthfully, as mysteries to each other, expressions of the wisdom and mystery of God. There is an old saying I have heard attributed to practically every religion: call God by whatever name you want, God's name is Truth. Perhaps it can also be said: call God by whatever name you wish, God's name is Mystery.

Practice

Reflect on times when you have stood at the gate of the tiger. Did you falter and back off? Did you pass through? What wisdom did you learn? Have you shared that insight and knowledge with others?

By baptism and confirmation, Christians believe that they have been given the gift of the Spirit called the fear of the Lord. Do you use this gift in your life for discerning what should be feared and what should not be feared? Or do you use it to come up with creative, courageous ways to face your fear or walk through your fears? Pick one of your fears and talk with others about this gift of fear of the Lord and how it can be used and given to others as gift so that fear does not overshadow our lives and stop our hearts. Work and pray that fear of the Lord might bring light, wisdom and light-heartedness to our world.

10 RIDING THE TIGER

> The world is too dangerous for anything but truth and too small for anything but love.[1]

At the end of the last chapter there was the story of 'The Tiger and the Persimmon'. There is more to that story. Once the tiger realised that the young child was not afraid of her, and that he obeyed his mother when he heard of this persimmon, she became afraid of the persimmon, though she had no idea what it actually was. The tiger slipped away from the hut and, still hungry, went to the pens to see if she could steal an ox or a goat for her dinner. It was pitch dark and as she slipped into the pen she did not notice that there was a thief already there, intent on stealing an ox too! This thief mistook the tiger for an ox and jumped on the tiger's back! The tiger was terrified and ran out of the pen, heading back towards the jungle. The tiger kept thinking, 'This must be that terrible persimmon that the boy was so afraid of'. She kept running hard, trying to shake the thief off. The thief held on tightly – he didn't want to get caught and was amazed that an ox could run so fast when it was afraid. When it grew lighter the thief realised that what he was riding and clinging to was a tiger and he was horrified! He let go and fell off the tiger, but the tiger never looked back – she headed back into the mountainous jungle, looking for her home and her children. She would have a story to tell them –

1. William Sloane Coffin.

about this ferocious thing she had heard of and escaped from, called a persimmon.

It is a story that makes us laugh and yet it is sobering. It tells us far too much of the truth of our own lives. We can be either the tiger or the thief in our relations and dealings with others. Both are deluded. Both live in fear. Both don't want to get caught – by others, the villager stealing – or by what the tiger thinks is awful, a persimmon. One at least realises what he did in the dark and that he survived to tell the tale. The tiger remains in ignorance and fear. Two very different forms of fear – one based on experience and a mistake, the other based on an experience and continued ignorance. Our own lives are filled with such moments. This is a story, but stories often mimic life and reveal deeper elements of life. This story keeps surprising us, throwing us off – with each bit of information our response changes but very little is bound up with what is actually reality. Flannery O'Connor was a remarkable novelist who died in her thirties. She spoke much about stories, about life and about how grace is always found in both. She writes:

> Story-writers are always talking about what makes a story work … From my own experience in trying to make stories 'work', I have discovered that what is needed is an action that is totally unexpected, yet totally believable, and I have found that, for me, this is always an action which indicates that grace has been offered. And frequently it is an action in which the devil has been the unwilling instrument of grace. This is not a piece of knowledge that I consciously put into my stories, it is a discovery that I get out of them.[2]

There is always grace. In the Scriptures the words 'grace', 'favour' and 'Spirit' are almost interchangeable. Grace is a divine saving and strengthening influence. Outside of theological definitions the word means courteous good will,

2. *Mystery and Manners*, Flannery O'Connor, Farrar, Straus, Giroux, 1961, p. 118.

attractiveness in posture or movement, elegance, a delay granted as a favour, even a prayer of thanksgiving, especially before meals. 'To grace' means to enhance, to confer honour and dignity upon. It is a synonym for forgiveness, compassion, mercy, charity, blessing and prayer. In a sense we live by grace, as we dwell in mystery and the universe bends towards gracefulness no matter the situation or the persons involved. As Flannery O'Connor learned in her writing, it was often the devil that was the unwilling instrument of such favour. The word 'devil' means literally the hinderer or antagonist, someone or anything that hinders us from being human and living religiously as the beloved of God. Any one of us may have been such an unwitting 'devil' or hinderer, causing agitation or violence to others or being the source of others becoming anxious or afraid. And yet, everything is redeemable, everything bears the possibility of transformation and holiness.

A friend of mine spent many months in El Salvador. He tells the story of a woman called Lucia Olmeida de Vasquez in Suchitoto, who gave him a line that he has held onto: 'They came and took away our fear.' She and her family and friends had lived through and survived running from the military, deaths of family members, being picked up by the military and living in a refugee camp. They all later returned to their homes and were subject to the military and the guerrillas passing through. Life was precarious. They were reluctant to get involved in anything with the Church or with their neighbours. But then some outsiders, four missionaries, came and they stayed to work, encouraging the people to get involved, to teach and to lead celebrations. She said: 'They came and took away our fear.' It was their presence that gave her the courage to begin again to really live and work with others. It is the presence of others – solidarity – that helps to cast out fear. Love casts out fear! The witness of courageous ordinary people helps to undermine fear.[3]

3. With thanks to John Donaghy, notes from El Salvador.

As long as we only individually try to face our fears we are limited in what we can do. We have our blindness, our prejudices, our ignorance, our experiences and biased assumptions, and our own weaknesses that impede us. To be human is to be in relation, to be in community and in order to be freed from our fears we absolutely need the presence and the courage of others with us. All the things we have looked at in this book are hard issues, massive realities in a world that is full of valid reasons to be fearful and worse, a world where many seek to use fear to control others and to get what they want. To face our fears is a two-fold endeavour of resistance and courage. Both transform us, others and our realities; both are ongoing and have their moments of intensity along with daily endurance that says, 'No that is not so'.

In his book, *Bread and Wine*, in *The Abruzzo Trilogy*, Ignazio Silone tells a story of a man, just one, who resists the dictatorship. He is a communist disguised as a priest (Don Paulo) and he goes out one night and writes anti-war slogans and the word 'No' on the walls of the town. It creates terror among the authorities. The priest talks with a young girl and says that if one person can say 'No', 'the whole of that formidable granite order is imperilled'. She asks: 'And if they catch him and kill him?' 'Killing a man who says "No" is a risky business,' said the priest. 'Even a corpse can go on whispering "no", "no", "no" with the tenacity and obstinacy that is peculiar to certain corpses. How can you silence a corpse ...'[4] He continues after a short pause:

> I too in the depth of my affliction have asked, where then is the Lord and why has He abandoned us? The loudspeakers and the bells that announced the beginning of the new butchery [the war against Ethiopia/Abyssinia] to the whole country were certainly not the voice of the Lord. Nor are the shelling and bombing of the Abyssinian villages that are reported

4. *The Abruzzo Trilogy: Bread and Wine*, Ignazio Silone, Zoland Books, 2000, p. 398.

daily in the press. But if a poor man alone in a hostile village gets up at night and scrawls with a piece of charcoal or paints DOWN WITH THE WAR on the walls the Lord is undoubtedly present. How is it possible not to see that behind that unarmed man in his contempt for danger, in his love for the so-called enemy, there is a direct reflection of the divine light? Thus, if simple workers are condemned by the Special Tribunal for similar reasons, there's no doubt about which side God is on.[5]

These words echo a Jewish Rabbi who wrote:

> The light of the Infinite One is without form and only takes shape – for good or bad – in the recipient. Therefore it is up to us. We have to do our best to shape God's light into blessing, not curse. For believers in God, our basic choice is to live in the freedom of the children of God or to live enslaved to fear and terror. The salvation of the world depends on it.

And these words all echo the words of Jesus on the night he was betrayed by one of his own and led off to be tortured, crucified, rejected and butchered, only to rise again. In John's gospel it is put so clearly so that we can take heart from his words:

> I have told you this while I am with you. The Advocate, the Holy Spirit that the Father will send in my name – he will teach you everything and remind you of all that I told you. Peace I leave with you, my peace I give to you. Not as the world gives do I give it to you. Do not let your hearts be troubled or afraid. You heard me tell you, 'I am going away and I will come back to you'. If you loved me, you would rejoice that I am going to the

5. Ibid., p. 413–4.

Father; for the Father is greater than I. And now I have told you this before it happens, so that when it happens you may believe. I will no longer speak much with you, for the ruler of the world is coming. He has no power over me, but the world must know that I love the Father and that I do just as the Father has commanded me to do. Get up, let us go.[6]

We hear those ringing words at every liturgy: 'Peace I leave with you, my peace I give to you. Not as the world gives do I give it to you.' 'Do not let your hearts be troubled or afraid.' These words are found deeply embedded in Jesus' last will and testament to his beloved friends. His parting gift is peace. It is a holy peace that casts out fear, transforms fear and is another form of peace to the ones that the world talks about – peace that comes at the end of a gun or a bomb. It is not peace that is a lull between ferocious battles, or peace where one group stops fighting and another picks up the weapons. It is not the peace of domination that is enforced by a greater power on a lesser group. It is not the peace that says we have to do this for our own protection, safety or security. It is not the peace that kills or allows others to kill and says, 'Wait, let the killing and the bombing go on a little longer – until they know we mean business'. It is not the peace of death, of silence with nothing left to plunder or destroy.

Jesus' peace is born of forgiveness, reconciliation, abiding justice, restitution and undoing the harm we have done to others and our world. Jesus' peace is expressed in making enemies into friends and kin, as close if not closer than family. Jesus' peace is not partial – it is universal in his embrace – no one is excluded. Jesus' peace endures long in the face of pain, fear, loneliness, rejection, even war, persecution and death.

Jesus' peace is an expression of truthfulness, of integrity, of courage and love. Jesus' peace is his own person, his words and his presence. We do not live spurred on by fear. We live

6. Jn 14:25-31.

engaged with making peace, with being peace-makers. The opposite of fear is courage. The opposite of terror is love. The opposite of being afraid is being a peace-maker. It is a gift given – and as it is received, it must be given again and again.

Jesus spoke these words with the darkness outside awaiting him and the darkness of even his own followers all around him. He spoke them in spite of his own fears of what others would do to him. He was not unrealistic, but aware of others' ability to do harm and inflict pain. Yet he gathered his soul and gave it to his friends as the gift of peace. Jesus seeks to realistically confront his own disciples with the harshness of what is going to happen to him, as it happened in one form or another to every prophet, to everyone who begged to differ with the dominant powers and say: 'No. No, I will not live in fear. I live in love. I live in grace.' And it is nothing like what masquerades in the world as what is necessary for security, safety, being a good citizen or sometimes even a good believer.

There is a children's story from southwest China called 'The Tiger in Court' that can present us with how strange this 'otherness of the peace of Jesus' is and yet it confirms in us the choice that we must make if we are not to be imprisoned in our fears.

Once upon a time there was an old, old woman. She had only one son and her husband had died long ago. One day, the son was hunting in the hills and he was attacked and eaten by a tiger. The woman was bereft, angry and paralysed by her loss. How would she live? Who would care for her? She was, everyone soon thought, utterly deranged. She didn't know what to do so she went to the local judge and demanded that the tiger be brought to justice. The judge could not get rid of her. The people listening stopped laughing when she continued to wail and grieve and demand that something be done.

The judge finally decided to do something for her. He told her that the tiger would be caught and brought to the court and amends would be made, somehow. Finally she stopped

screaming and waited for her day in the court. Now it was the
judge's problem. How could he get someone to go and 'arrest'
the tiger? Tigers were nearly impossible to catch alive. He
summoned all his clerks and workers and put the problem
before them. As chance would have it, one of the clerks was
roaring drunk and he volunteered to go and get the tiger! The
judge issued a warrant and wondered what in the world would
happen next. Meanwhile the clerk, Li Neng, began to sober up
and realised he was now in trouble. He went off and rounded
up his friends, many of whom were hunters, and bribed them
into coming with him to arrest the tiger – they could not kill
him. They searched for days and no tiger was to be found.

After weeks of fruitless searching he returned to the judge
and the judge had him beaten for his failure. In misery, poor Li
Neng went to the great Cheng-huang temple and prostrated
himself, praying desperately. While he prayed a tiger
approached, walked into the temple and sat by the doorway.
Lin Neng was terrified. The tiger didn't move and neither did
Li Neng. Time passed. Finally, Li Neng turned to the tiger
who was looking straight at him and spoke: 'If you are the tiger
who killed that poor old widow's son, you know you need to do
restitution. If you are that tiger, let me bind you with a rope
and bring you to the judge.' Stunned, he watched while the
tiger lowered his head and murmured a low growl that
sounded like submission. Li Neng, moved slowly and, even in
his fear, had the wits to go and get a rope and throw it over the
tiger's head. He walked out of the temple with the tiger on his
leash.

Li Neng walked straight away to the judge's court. The
judge was terrified and babbled out: 'Did you kill and eat the
widow's son?' The tiger nodded his head. The judge tried to
pull himself together. He knew the law and spoke: 'It has never
been the law of this land to kill anyone who murders, so you
will not be killed. But there must be justice. You ate the
widow's only son. You will live, but you must now act as

though you are the widow's only son. If you do this, you will be exonerated.' The tiger bowed his head again. The judge looked at Li Neng and signalled that he was to take the tiger outside and let him go. Li Neng led the tiger outside the village and carefully slipped the rope loose. The tiger walked away. The widow heard what happened and was furious. She wanted that tiger killed for killing her son. She raved about the judge's corruptness and cowardice. But the next morning when she opened her front door, on the stones before her was a dead deer. She took it inside, skinned it, preparing the meat and took the skin to sell. She used every part of the deer, bartering for what she needed. When she needed more food or something for her survival, there was another animal on her doorstep: another deer, rabbits, wild sheep or goats, even wild plants and vegetables. Sometimes there was a piece of jewellery or money – scavenged from the trail or found. She had what she needed to live, and more besides.

Every morning when she got up, she went immediately to the front door. Sometimes it was empty and sometimes the tiger lay curled up at the end of the stones. He would often prowl around the house at night as though he were protecting her and he was never far, except when he was hunting. As time passed, the woman began to feel secure around the tiger and began to think of it as her protector.

The years passed and the old woman died. The villagers gathered to wail and grieve her before burying her and while they were sounding the gongs and chanting, the tiger came again. He stood in the doorway and roared and roared, and then turned and went away. When the old woman was buried the tiger returned and roared again. The mourners backed away and the tiger went up to her burial mound and lay down. They carefully finished the rituals and left. The tiger stayed all night and the next day and night, and then, pawing the ground, left. He was never seen again.

The people thought about the tiger who had submitted to

justice and who had cared for the woman so well and faithfully, even though he had been a tiger and was only doing what his nature demanded – finding food – when he had killed her son. The villagers decided to build a temple in the tiger's honour. The temple of the Faithful Tiger still stands today.

The story is told and people are reminded that even the most feared of the animals has it in their nature to nobly do what is right. If this is so, then what is to be expected of human beings who consider themselves superior to these creatures, the tigers?

Is the story fantasy? Is it impossible? Is it just fanciful? What is it telling us about ourselves – often tigers in our own ways? What are we capable of doing and being when we face our fears and live with courage and integrity? There is a prayer from the ancient church that is worth knowing and, once prayed, can come true in our lives:

> We thank you, O God, for the saints of all ages;
> For those who in times of darkness kept the lamp of faith burning;
> For the great souls who saw visions of larger truth and dared to declare it;
> For the multitude of quiet and gracious souls whose presence has purified and sanctified the world;
> And for those known and loved by us, who have passed from this earthly fellowship into the fuller light of life with you. Amen.[7]

Facing our fears, living with courage and using the powerful gift of peace that Jesus gives allows us the strength and the possibility of riding the tigers of our lives, not just by accident, but consciously. This courage of being the children of God makes us realise that we are, in the end, the tiger. There is the figure and symbol in the Old Testament of the Lion of Judah that we have attributed to Jesus ... perhaps Jesus is the Tiger

---

7. Anonymous, found in *Prayers of the Martyrs*, compiled and translated by Duane W.H. Arnold, Zondervan Publishing House, 1991, p. 110.

and we are the tiger's cubs learning to believe that we can face our fears and live together as a tribe of tigers intent on making the world a wild, fierce and wondrous place to dwell for all.

Patrick Kavanagh wrote that the resurrection is 'a laugh freed forever and ever …'. I have tried to find out if tigers laugh, smile, growl or rumble contentedly but there seems to be a dearth of material in this regard! But we are the children of the resurrection and it is our nature to laugh freed, for ever and ever … we do not have to wait until forever. It is our nature to face the tiger, to ride the tiger, to enter the tiger's gates and to be the tiger. We need to practise this alone and with others, sharing courage and wisdom together.

Four years ago I was reflecting on what happened on September 11, 2001 and how to live in the world that was now suffused with terror triggered by that event. I was also pondering a world that used that date and experience to do horror to others and to undo a great deal of the advances that the struggle for human rights, dignity and justice had so painstakingly accomplished. I wrote what follows and called it 'A New Vocation at 59'. Perhaps a more apt title would be 'I Vow to Be a Tiger.' It is a manifesto of sorts, a statement of courage and of peace in the face of fear and the horrors that fear helps us to perpetrate and excuse. Fear scars and tears at what it means to be human and to be the image of God for one another. We are not allowed to live in fear, to be ruled by fear and to use fear as an excuse for anything we do. We live with heart as human beings – we live with courage, with peace and with the Truth.

My Vow

Remembering that nothing really changed that particular day – we just didn't let the mystery of the Resurrection grasp hold of us in time. And so I vow ….

To dispel sorrow, with courage and humility and to show your best face – God's to all.

To begin: practise lingering and looking, though not just at what attracts, holes, spiralling stars spun of glory, morning stillness, a bloom past season, remembrance that tugs at both ache and unexpected goodness – but look too at things we resist: evil, greed, hatred, horror, burning flesh, lies (collateral damage), reports of depleted uranium left behind as a legacy of suffering – killing long after you've left black holes along with spiralling stars spun of glory

Next: be a bodhichetta, a bodhisattva (the goddess of compassion and mercy), practise diligent compassion standing and sitting and even sleeping. Pity the destruction, those destroyed and those intent on dominance and making havoc. Pity for lacking any sense of morals, decency and humanness.

Compassion: to only give what is needed to those lacking, and to ask them first.

Passion: for justice and truth and respect and to cherish them with all your strength. Even if all I can do is a fragment here and there, something that leaves a thin crack still visible in the repaired vase, or rearranging and culling the flowers to last a bit longer, still beautiful.

Then, no hindrance to hope, however weak and stumbling. Stir joy, seed it liberally, edge it with something protective, small like marigolds, but tough (looking through the lens of the long eye of the Divine). The only fence – arms entwined at that precise moment before the music starts and you must dance – all together.

Listen! Listen! (that means obey the others' deepest aspirations). We're all one already!
Life is dense. Strike deep with gentleness.
Oh then, the 'pièce de resistance' – forgiveness

The discipline: the atmosphere, like air necessary for survival and the only way that one day war will perish utterly and there will be no mourners, no wake, as earth awakes to life and recovery and children can breathe easy, now never having to know the call to kill. Even the trees will surge with growth, long stunted from hugging the ground (along with so many humans), hoping never to stand out – in someone's gun sights. How? Pray constantly so there is a reservoir of holiness to fall back on – divine resolves of Peace – spaciousness needs attentiveness. Provoke peace! Remember we are here to ward off killing and death. We are all supposed to die of old age.

Court dialogue and reconciliation. Never, ever let two sides, two people, two groups, two nations stop talking or walk away – never! Remember: grace is unlimited and actual.

So – no cynicism, scepticism; no belittling, moaning, groaning, whinging and whining.
Keep in mind the best interests of others (not yours). Leap ahead – avert conflict.

Renew your commitment to forgiveness with constant attentiveness to its reality (from God in your life, our lives). And then when it all seems to fall apart, there are last-ditch interfaces.

Try unstoppable weeping – know your weaknesses. Be kind to them, generous to all. In a bind, offer dinner at your place to all involved. No grasping – at any specific outcome. Be prepared to ad lib, innovate, let go of anything not essential. Trust – rely on humanity's possibility for sheer goodness and don't underestimate resurrection now/here.

Don't clench – fingers, face, teeth, hope, words (no harm – no violence in this place).

Get a degree in compromise. Minor in risk-taking. Dissertation studies – hope against hope. Last resort – take a break. Break out in laughter, hum, sing along, everybody shut up, put on the music, take your shoes off. Do something gentle as antidote to stalemate. Or, like in Japan, everybody go sit in a hot tub, naked, so everyone in the discussion no longer has a table and suits and titles between them – there's nothing between them.

If it rains outside – stop, go out – it's a blessing in most indigenous communities.

If it snows – even better – it's God's gracious comforter falling over the earth, time for a nap. Plain old glorious sunshine: stand, faces tilted backwards and up and tell yourself again the ancient words: 'The Holy One lets the sun to shine on the just and the unjust alike!' Clouds – transition time, interludes. It will pass – figure out, like children what they really might be up there – the art of cloud deciphering is akin to diplomacy. Whatever, hang on for a dearer life. Everything dies. Everything goes through conversion.

Ground rule – Love: love profoundly. Love indiscriminately. Just love. Practise embracing the other, even in your head. Imagination stretches, frees and reveals. We are made in the image and likenesses of the Holy Ones. That was just for starters – now we are made in the image of the Trinity, the Trice Holy Community. As Merton said: 'We are already one, we just have to remember that.' We must let that innate radiance within show forth. That is the only Epiphany – the showing forth of Peace on earth, living and dwelling among us. And so, coming and going, we must bow deeply before the other – one never really knows who one bows before.

P.S. It's a marathon. Pace yourself. At times plod mindlessly. Let your body take over, while the spirit lags and regroups.

P.P.S. If you can't sustain joy, settle for gladness. Take a nap, get over it (as the kids say). Have a glass of wine, or two (for the heart), practicsing toasting life and peace on earth – God is with us and mercy and favour are hidden among every one of us, especially among those we'd all too quickly call 'enemy' instead of learning their name, their nicknames and what those who love call them in moments of tenderness.

This is where it begins again. This is the hour of the Tiger. It is time to face our fears and more – it is the hour of courage, of the Truth and of love – the hour of the Tiger, the hour of integrity when we become what we were dreamed of by the Holy One. Come, tigers, let us go from here.

Practice
Write your own vow – of how to be a tiger in your world. Then share it with others. Make a list of tigers who will stay together and face whatever fears there are together. Pray to the Lord of all, God's Tiger, Jesus, who sees us as cubs learning the truth of what it means to be a tiger.

BIBLIOGRAPHY

Books consulted as background and quoted.

The Life of Columba by Adamnan, abridged translation John Gregory, Floris Books, Edinburgh, Scotland, 1999.

The No-Nonsene Guide to Terrorism, Jonathan Barker, New Internationalist Publications, Oxford, 2003.

Fear: A Cultural History, Joanna Bourke, Shoemaker and Hoard, an imprint of Avalon Publishing Group, Inc., Emeryville, CA, 2005.

At Peace and Unafraid: Public Order, Security and the Wisdom of the Cross, edited by Duane K. Friesen and Gerald W. Schlabach, Herald Press, Scottdale, PA, 2005.

Left to Tell: Discovering God Amidst the Rwandan Holocast, Immaculee Ilibagiza, with Steve Erwin, Hay House, Inc., Carlsbad, CA/UK, 2006.

In a Dark Time: Images for Survival, edited by Robert Jay Lifton and Nicholas Humphrey, Harvard University Press, Cambridge, MA, 1984.

The Horrors we Bless: Rethinking the Just-War Legacy, Daniel C. Maguire, Fortress Press, Minneapolis, MN, 2007.

In the End – The Beginning: The Life of Hope, Jurgen Moltmann, translated Margaret Kohl, Fortress Press, Minneapolis, MN, 2004.

Where is God? Earthquake, Terrorism, Barbarity, and Hope, Jon Sobrino, Orbis Books, Maryknoll, NY, 2004.

The Mystery of Death, Dorothee Soelle, translation Nancy Lukens-Rumscheidt and Martin Lukens-Rumscheidt, Fortress Press, Minneapolis, MN, 2007.

Anger: The Seven Deadly Sins, Robert A.F. Thurman, Oxford University Press, NY, 2005.

The End of Memory: Remembering Rightly in a Violent World, Miroslav Volf, Wm. B. Eerdmans Publishing Company, Grand Rapids, Michigan/Cambridge, UK, 2006.

The Monastic Way: Ancient Wisdom for Contemporary Living: A Book of Daily Readings, ed. Hannah Ward and Jennifer Wild, Canterbury Press, Norwich, UK, 2006.

The Truce of God, Rowan Williams, Wm. B. Eerdmans Publishing Company, Grand Rapids, Michigan/Cambridge, UK, 2005.

Floating takes Faith: Ancient Wisdom for a Modern World, Rabbi David J. Wolpe, Behrman House, www.behrmanhouse.com, NJ, 2004.

The Violence of God and the War of Terror, Jeremy Young, Darton, Longman and Todd, UK, 2007.

CHILDREN'S BOOKS

One Hand Clapping: Zen Stories for all Ages, selected, adapted and retold by Rafe Martin and Manuela Soares, Rizzoli, NY, 1995.

Bring Back the Deer, Jeffrey Prusski, Gulliver Books, Harcourt Brace Jovanovich, San Diego, CA, 1988.

The Nightwalker, Richard Thompson, Fitzhenry & Whiteside, Ontario, Canada, 2002.

The Legend of the Chinese Zodiac, Susan Whitfield & Philippa-Alys Browne, Barefoot Books, Bristol, UK, 1992.